the Je

a Rebellious M

MW00848869

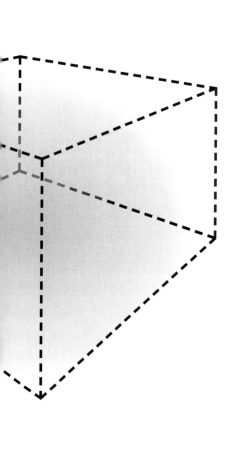

the Jewish Prison
a Rebellious Meditation on the State of Judaism
Jean Daniel

Translated by Charlotte Mandell

MELVILLE HOUSE PUBLISHING
HOBOKEN, NEW JERSEY

©2005 Melville House Publishing

Originally published in French as:
La prison juive
©2003 Editions Odile Jacob

Publication of this book was assisted by the
French Ministry of Foreign Affairs and
the Cultural Service of the French Embassy.

Melville House Publishing
P.O. Box 3278
Hoboken, NJ 07030

Book design: David Konopka

First Edition
ISBN: 0-9761407-5-6

Library of Congress Cataloging-in-Publication Data
Daniel, Jean, 1920-
  [Prison juive. English]
  The Jewish prison : a rebellious meditation on the state of Judaism / Jean Daniel.
    p. cm.
  Includes bibliographical references.
  ISBN 0-9761407-6-4 (pbk.)
  1. Judaism--20th century. 2. Judaism and politics--France. 3. Religion--
Philosophy. I. Title.
  BM45.D3513 2005
  296--dc22
                                            2005002828

Table of Contents

vii

Table of Contents

the Jewish Prison

Jean Daniel

3

Author's Acknowledgements

I am indebted to Jean-François Colosimo for the skill and tact with which he encouraged and supported my project, and enriched it with his testimony.

Dominique-Adriana Desvigne and Véronique Cassarin-Grand had to endure my perfectionist anxieties, and did so heroically.

I must not forget either Georges Bensoussan or Henry Laurens; both could verify the benefit I drew from reading Bensoussan's study on Israel and Laurens' on the Palestinians.[1] But I fear that Bensoussan and Laurens will wind up in agreement against me, though their individual works would not seem to have encouraged such agreement.

---

[1] Georges Bensoussan, *Une histoire intellectuelle et politique du sionisme 1860-1940* (Paris: Fayard, February 2002); Henry Laurens, *La Question de la Palestine*: Vol. 1, *L'Invention de la Terre Sainte*; Vol. 2, *Une mission sacrée de civilisation* (Paris: Fayard, March 2002).

And the Lord said unto Satan, Whence comest thou? Then Satan answered the Lord, and said, From going to and fro in the earth, and from walking up and down in it. And the Lord said unto Satan, Hast thou considered my servant Job, that *there* is none like him in the earth, a perfect and an upright man, one that feareth God, and escheweth evil? Then Satan answered the Lord, and said, Doth Job fear God for nought? Hast not thou made an hedge about him, and about his house, and about all that he hath on every side?

The Book of Job 1:7-10,
King James Version

Introduction

He hath . . . set me up for his mark.

Job 16:12.

The idea that the Jews might actually have imposed on themselves a prison as their destiny and that they have offered the impossible magnitude of this fate to humanity came to me one day in Jerusalem. I was in conversation with a Dominican priest—a Zionist, incidentally—and with a pacifist Israeli teacher. It was the year 2000. They had just come back from Gaza shocked by the Palestinian suffering they had seen, but they made it clear that their indignant compassion had been, upon returning, dried up in their throats by the horrors of a suicide attack. How could either group ever forget what they had caused to be done to the other? The Jewish professor quoted Golda Meir: "We might someday forgive you for killing our children, but we will never forgive you for forcing us into the position of killing yours." The conversation should have continued normally, as it might have only a dozen years ago, with an inventory of the supposed causes for the tragedy. Causes that would have to do only with colonial economics, social issues, and history. At worst, we would

the Jewish Prison
Jean Daniel

have deplored the fact that, even in the Holy Land, man continues to be a wolf to man, and that as a Semite he is the worst enemy to his brother.

We would have regretted the fact that the Jews of Central Europe—the first great Europeans, according to Milan Kundera—were unable, or did not know how, to share their exceptional adventure with their neighbors. A flamboyant epic that included the resurrection of a language, Hebrew: a real cultural miracle. We would have wondered how these Jews for whom Judaism is *an ethics of law and justice* experienced the sufferings of the Palestinians and the anguish of the Israelis. On that point, we would have remained within the domain of ethics, of domestic and cultural issues, a domain dear to unbelieving dreamers and pioneers, heralds and heroes of the "Jewish State," according to the exact title of the foundational book by Theodor Herzl.

Alas, these regrets were no longer appropriate. Nor were our hopes that monotheistic brotherhood might temper nationalistic excesses. None of that was possible anymore, as soon as we heard the shouts of the Jewish "settlers" invoking divine will, and as soon as we saw them occupy Palestinian lands, and as soon as we saw the fury of the kamikazes disguised as instruments of the same divine will aim at attaining sainthood by murdering civilians and committing suicide.

But it is precisely these settlers who, *nolens volens*, after their disastrous "settlements," have aroused in the Palestinians the feeling of unbearable humiliation. And it is also these kamikazes who have provoked the "holy alliance" of Israelis rallying round Sharon and who have defused the forces of peace in Israel. The idolaters in both camps have ended up starting a real war of religions. There was no choice then but to note that the Israeli-Palestinian conflict, prolonged by Judeo-Arab antagonism, was in the process of undergoing a *negative theologization*. Primacy was accorded to the theological explanation in its most fanatical version. Suddenly, it seemed natural to us, to this Dominican, the professor, and myself, to look for an explanation of the conflict in the interpretations of sacred texts. It struck me that this was a very serious matter and that a radical change had occurred. Without batting an eyelid we abandoned the realm of politics and went to look in Heaven for reasons for continuing to confront each other.

This shift from the political to the religious, from the rational to the theological, is too weighted with tragedy for me not to linger over it. In the conflicts that make up the history of mankind, those who study war distinguish wars in which the protagonists kill each other until they beg for truce or till the defeat of one of them, wars in which external powers impose a peace on the fighting parties, and, finally, wars in which the conquerors end up occupying the territory of the conquered. To explain the conditions of the conflict, the history of peoples, the strength of their firepower, laws are usually evoked. But no one thought about God in interpreting Verdun, Pearl Harbor, or Stalingrad. In fact, we had to wait till the attacks of 2001 on the World Trade Center towers, with its spirit of the Crusades—and praise of sacrificial murder—to rediscover the charter of the order of the Templars bestowed by "Father Bernard, abbot of Clairvaux," at the time of the Frankish kingdom of Jerusalem. Thus we abandoned the ground of reason, so reassuring beneath our feet, for dreamlike journeys into the convolutions of theology.

But what is theological thinking? It is the way of all those who have not followed, or who have abandoned, the paths of Hellenic and critical thought, those, in other words, who think that everything begins with a Revelation. I have recalled in a book, *Dieu est-il fanatique?*, how the two Cordovans, doctors and philosophers, Averroes and Maimonides, agreed with Thomas of Aquinas, "in the manner of Aristotle," to reconcile faith and reason. They could not have done more at that time. But they showed how belief in revelation would not allow thought to be completely free. In fact, they did not want it to be free for ordinary mortals. But they did contribute in large part to unlacing the straitjacket of theological thought. And it is to this straitjacket that the noblest and freest minds have invited us today to return.

As Emmanuel Levinas writes in *Difficult Freedom*:

> *As the source of the great monotheistic religions*
> *to which the world owes as much as it does to*
> *ancient Greece and Rome, Judaism is a vital*
> *part of living actuality through its contribu-*
> *tions of ideas and texts by men and women*
> *who, as pioneers of great ventures and as*
> *victims of the great cataclysms of history, are*
> *linked in a direct and uninterrupted lineage to*
> *the people of sacred history. The attempt to*
> *revive a state in Palestine, and to rediscover*
> *universally relevant creative inspirations from*
> *long ago, cannot be conceived of without*
> *reference to the Bible.*

This is magnificent—and tragic. For Emmanuel Levinas will question himself later on about the price of this *resurrection* of a State in Palestine. While still admitting that everything is there...

I am not a theologian and have no taste for being one, far from it. But the fact remains that my unbelief has remained religious, and my sensitivity to the masterpieces of universal literature, in this case the Bible, has predisposed me towards an immersion in this universe of a pre-Islamic *Thousand and One Nights* told by the Jews and the first Christians. But, starting from the moment when these tales leave the realm of myth and miracle to constitute the ethical codes that will have an overwhelming worldly and political influence, then we should indeed try to put ourselves in the mindframe of those who believe in them.

We know that upon their arrival in 1910, the Jews found settled and highly structured populations, whereas they had imagined they could take root again in "a land without people for a people without land." They were forced, then, to transform their vision, their objectives, and their strategy. Without wanting to (and even, sometimes, for some of them, against their own will) they had to appeal somewhere beyond the hostility of the Arab world and international law for a higher legitimacy that permitted them to wage war. If they were in Palestine, they told themselves, it was not by chance. A force had led them there, one to which they did not yet dare give the name of God, a force of which they were discovering they were already the prisoners. And, after the Shoah of course, but especially after the victory of 1967, they did nothing but glorify their prison.

But the people in question, the Palestinian people, turned out to be valorous, intensely dignified in their suffering, outraged at the fate imposed on them, determined to make themselves into a nation, that is to say, to resist getting from Israel what they had so painfully endured from their Arab brothers, as well as from the Turkish,

English, and Jordanian occupiers. Thus the great scholar Yeshayahou Leibowitz told me, in December 1992: "The Palestinians, opposed to the offer of sharing and peace, can be considered responsible for the war of 1948 and its consequences. But from 1967 on, the Israelis are responsible for all that has followed, and thus for our impossible situation as occupiers."

Before our conversation broke up, the priest and the teacher had agreed that as long as mankind has been mankind there has only been one interesting problem, the problem of Evil. This evades the issue. It was easy to agree to it, in the place where we were, during the time we were speaking, and while we were witnessing the disasters of a fratricidal conflict on a land sanctified by two peoples torn apart. There is one single answer, said the Dominican: It was given by the Palestinian Jew Jesus, on the Cross. He added that the Shoah could be thought of as an identical Passion. This was a point of view that a thinker as profoundly Jewish as Emmanuel Levinas came to share.

My answer I found only later on. I give it today. First of all Jesus. The only cry from him, which, at bottom, ever truly moved me deeply, is his question: "Father, why have You abandoned me?" For in these words there is nothing more than a man cast into solitariness by a non-incarnate, omnipotent God who could not abandon the child He gave himself. This cry resounds in my ears, since I seem to have heard it as the cry of a Jewish rebel who gives expression to all the rebels of the world since the Creation. Yes, he is only a man among men, and, on his Cross, he has no thought of a resurrection or even, it seems, of pity. All that he has preached to others, he cannot put in practice. He thinks he is chained to a god whom he may have invented and who escapes him. He had thought he was a Chosen One. He is only an orphan. He is treated like a Prometheus guilty of trying to steal, not progress, but holiness from Heaven.

Each time I leaf through the big book devoted to Gothic art published by Mazenod, I stop short before a Christ on the cross, a woodcarving from the twelfth century owned by the Bresset Collection, but I've never known where one could go to admire it. In any case it is immediately apparent that it's a very pure masterpiece. And what made me linger over it, and what makes me mention it here, is the unexpected expression of the face (a detail is given on a subsequent page). Christ has a look that's more overwhelmed than suffering; he lets his gaze fall on his wounded body with a gravity that I would like to think is accusatory—"Look at your work," he says to God, it seems to me, or "Why did I believe in You?" There is in the second movement of Handel's *Messiah* certain musical phrases that could serve as a caption in sound, that we should listen to when contemplating this Gothic sculpture.

To tell the truth, since I've known that, since the time I decided to understand the Passion in that way, this man, Jesus, has been as close to me as the most brotherly of brothers, like the one I find in so many passages from the majestic *Book of Job*. This Jesus is, just like Job, a victim, a Just Man; nothing tells us that he understands the enormity of his misfortune while he does nothing but good. None of the great painters who claimed to be intercessors of divine grace in their art were tempted to make the Passion into an ecstasy, or even to show a being who was indeed suffering, but who was waiting with confidence for his resurrection, the secret of which he held.

In any case, if Golgotha signifies a sharing of martyrdom, all the Golgothas of Auschwitz could not convey this sharing. The Holocaust weighs in such a crushing way on us that a number of Jewish thinkers, and just as many Christians—their minds determined to rescue faith from all the doubts that reason imposes and legitimizes—end up declaring that God, this God of Abraham, Moses, and Jesus, this God of Augustine, who created Time and History and who gave a meaning to life, must be absent from History and Time to remain innocent in His eternity. Feeble strategem! Miserable panacea! Over all these new God-fearing people who, each in his own Church, have the impudence of founding and preserving their faith on something other than anxiety and questioning, over all those who want at any price and in any manner to make the mysteries of Life and of Evil enter into a convenient arrangement, we should choose controversy.

I resigned myself to concluding that the Shoah, a monstrosity that the Jews have purposefully decided to think of as being as unique as the god invented by Moses, poses a radically new problem. As a friend said: "The black sun of the Shoah burned everything—the dreams of long ago as well as the rationality of today." The fact remains that, to understand it and acknowledge it, the distinction between faith and reason is quickly revealed to be insufficient. The *credo quia absurdum* has its limits. So the temptation is great for a believer who clings to his faith to leave God outside the absurd. But this is not possible. And it would be too easy.

Others, we know, see on the contrary a punitive project in the genocide, a new Flood, reminding the Jews of their radical, fundamental, identity-founding difference. A way, for instance, of condemning the assimilation that was underway, and that would have meant the disappearance of a people whose existence was decided by God. By this reckoning, Hitler, in trying to exterminate all the Jews, assured the survival of a few. This is an unbearable imputation. All the more so since, from such a perspective, one risks having to conclude that, after tragically failing in their wish to be individuals like other people, the Jews are today frustrated in their desire to constitute a State like other people. And that is also impossible, as we will see further on.

Let us cite the most edifying example of assimilation: that of Germany, which fascinated humanity with its musicians and philosophers, and which wanted to exterminate its own citizens. Einstein, Mahler, Freud, and Kafka are contemporaries of Hitler. They came from the same society. Despite the number and celebrity of converts to Christianity (Husserl, Mahler, but also Schönberg, who however was to re-convert back to Judaism after the Shoah), German Jewish populations never really erased their origins. The rise of Nazism coincided with the affirmation of an intelligentsia that boasted of a perfectly Germanicized Jewishness. In 1942, Stefan Zweig killed himself in Brazil because of—among other things—the conflict that his thwarted love for the German language aroused in him. That same year the Jewish Carmelite, Edith Stein, who had converted before she was deported and gassed, accepted her death "with submission" for—among other things—"the salvation of Germany." Nahum Goldman, the first president of the World Jewish Congress, went so far as to wonder if there wasn't, at bottom, an identical destiny shared by the German people and the Jewish people.

But there was indeed the Shoah, and now we find ourselves, after this scandalous ordeal, in the pathos of

the Jewish Prison
Jean Daniel

Israeli-Palestinian convulsions. The Jewish philosopher Martin Buber recalled that "there will obviously be no legitimacy for the Hebrew State unless it makes itself accepted by all its neighbors." This is what Simone Weil says of conquests: "None is acceptable except one that allows settlers to be one with natives." But, condemned to aggression by the famous "Arab refusal," how could this little State make itself accepted without imposing itself with armed force? That was the trap. By being faithful to the Covenant that advocated a return to Zion, they became unfaithful to the injunction to be nothing but priests and witnesses.

It was all these contradictions brought to the point of white-hot tensions that inspired in me the feeling, suddenly clear and obvious, that the Jews had deliberately locked themselves up in a veritable prison, one they passionately loved. In the end, they came to see in this confinement of the chosen people the servitude and greatness of the Jewish condition. They had made this decision themselves, but how could it be foreign to God's designs? How could it not have begun with the first divine caprice, which involved the command to Abraham to leave everything, to abandon everything, to uproot himself in order to take root elsewhere, without any explanation about the chosen place?

The prison could indeed have various structures, but the Jews found, in their joyful distress, that each time they tried to escape, a force recaptured them to punish them and reinstate them, in pride and misery, in their captive condition.

This idea embarrasses even me. Israel as a prison? Just because its people have not disappeared? Because it is miraculous that it has survived so many persecutions? Because it incarnates hope instead of believing in its curse? What about the Armenians? And the Kurds? And the Polish people, erased from the map three times? What about the black Africans, for centuries imprisoned in slavery? In fact, it was obviously not so simple. And the prison, of course, is elsewhere. It is in the minds of those people, even unbelievers, who act as if their jailer could be none other than God, whether it's in the Holy Land or in the diaspora.

But what explains this behavior? I thought I found the answer when I collided, so to speak, with the inaugural, founding concepts of Election and of the Covenant in the first chapters of the Hebrew Bible. In this kind of premonitory illumination, I told myself that all humanity would, one day or another, be invited to join the Jews in prison. And that they would be no happier there. It remained for me to wonder, in the most rational and, if possible, coldest way, what the reasons could be for this strange Jewish questioning that, since the time of the Covenants with Noah, then with Abraham, and finally with Moses, and especially since the time of the Shoah and the State of Israel, feeds the collective imagination of so many millions of people who should be indifferent. We have seen earlier, and we will see more clearly later on, what the traumatism of the Shoah had been. But what relationship could that have with the creation of the State of Israel? That is what will concern us.

In the 1950's, some great Catholic writers, from Jacques Maritain to Paul Claudel, went so far as to say, after Léon Bloy, that "the Jews constrain humanity's route as a dike bars the course of a river: to raise its level." And the Shoah was, according to them, the proof of this. This messianic devotion was, perhaps, based on a conscience made guilty by the former crimes of their Church. It implied, especially in Claudel, the idea that God, through genocide, had solemnly and tempestuously charged His people with precipitating its return to the Land promised to Abraham. "You no longer have the right to wait," said Claudel to his Jewish friends. Addressing Israel in his famous style, the great Catholic poet wrote: "God did not spend so much time getting used to your interesting physiognomy only to deprive himself, all of a sudden, of the benefits of your curious calling and your personality. It's not every day that you find a people like Israel to work with." In fact Claudel's genuine compassion for the victims of the genocide was inseparable from the role the most liberal Christians assigned to the Jews: that of being the most faithful witnesses to the passion of Jesus. But also perhaps the blindest. The fact remains that neither Claudel, nor Maritain, nor their Jewish interlocutors could foresee what we are observing today, in the margins of the prodigious expansion of Islam, namely: the exceptional centrality of Jewish thought and its influence on the United States and on the entire world.

To tell the truth, the novel intensity of the repercussions of the most monstrous genocide in History—the one to which people consciously decided to give a name (the Shoah)—and the ethnic-religious and almost global geopolitical after-effects of the Israeli-Palestinian conflict, these two facts, can lead us to believe that meditating on the Jewish question amounts to meditating, now in 2003, on the human condition itself.

The Biblical Exception

There are of course studies, passionately disputed but edifying at times, that place Bolshevik and Nazi atrocities on the same plane, or reckon colonialism as equivalent to the other two genocidal enterprises. This is an endless discussion that can divide honest men, and I have experienced difficulty dealing with this subject during long conversations with my friend, the historian François Furet.

Is it enough to tally up the millions of victims of this or that genocide? Does the notion of a single totalitarianism contrive to triumph over the diversity of its manifestations? Should we, with Hannah Arendt, cling to the thesis of the banality of evil and the interchangeability of victims? So many questions, and I want to leave them open for the moment. But the fact remains that no one has wondered if it was possible to "think after the gulag," as Emil Fackenheim wondered how we could "think after Auschwitz." Or as a religious thinker, Hans Jonas, wondered what *the concept of God after Auschwitz* becomes. No one has asked himself the question of the absence of God during the forced migrations and massacres of populations in the Soviet Union, or after the Cambodian genocide, or after these recent—and terrifying—genocides in Rwanda. We have seen how certain Jewish thinkers declared themselves reconciled to the absence of God. But others have made another cry heard, according to which one cannot endure being *guilty for having been born* (Simone Lagrange). I have already cited those thinkers who had determined to justify the wrath of this God whose mercy is supposed to be infinite. The Creator, according to them, was terribly disappointed with His creatures, even more than before the Flood, which, we remember, was not supposed to come again according to the Promise made to Noah. They evidently think that God is never so present as when He condemns, punishes, and decimates peoples that are "necessarily" guilty. The specific cruelty of the Shoah would emphasize, in this case, only the exceptional unworthiness of the sinners. That is the thesis of divine punishment that, since the time of the destruction of Sodom and Gomorrah, since the destruction of the two Temples and the various exoduses, is regularly brandished to justify divine cruelty and to summon the faithful to contrition and purification.

Reading the
Two Testaments
Deuteronomy prophesies: "If thou wilt not observe to do all the words of this law [concerning the land of Canaan]...so the Lord will rejoice over you to destroy you, and to bring you to nought; and ye shall be plucked from off the land whither thou goest to possess it" (Deut. 28:58, 63). And Jeremiah prophesies the ordeal of exile: "Like as ye have forsaken me, and served strange gods in your land, so shall ye serve strangers in a land *that* is not yours" (Jer. 5:19). But later on, the same Jeremiah who lived in Jerusalem in the Sixth Century B.C., during the period that followed the first offensive of Nebuchadnezzar, while the kingdom of Judea was only an autonomous Babylonian territory, Jeremiah himself, then, addresses a letter to the Judeans who had been deported to Babylon. He says to them: "Build ye houses, and dwell *in them*; and plant gardens, and eat the fruit of them; Take ye wives, and beget sons and daughters; and take wives for your sons, and give your daughters to husbands, that they may bear sons and daughters; that ye may be increased there, and not diminished. And seek the peace of the city whither I have caused you to be carried away captives, and pray unto the Lord for it: for in the peace thereof shall ye have peace" (Jer. 29:5-7).

the Jewish Prison
Jean Daniel

Extraordinary message, superb and noble ambiguity of Jeremiah; it is not exile that counts, it is what one makes of it. You can be faithful to the concept of Election (if not to the Covenant!) wherever you are, as Théo Klein reminds us. The followers of both of these schools have equal authority in Israel.

Except that by being made into a punishment, one just more implacable than all the others, the Shoah loses its precious uniqueness and even its singularity. In any case, can the very idea of a punishment keep any meaning when it is manifested not by the punishment of the guilty, but by the punishment of the whole community? From the point of view of Jewish morality, even the thinkers of the post-Babylonian era, Jeremiah, Ezekiel, and others had vociferously denounced this concept: "What mean ye, that ye use this proverb concerning the land of Israel, saying, The fathers have eaten sour grapes, and the children's teeth are set on edge? *As* I live, saith the Lord GOD, ye shall not have *occasion* any more to use this proverb in Israel. Behold, all souls are mine; as the soul of the father, so also the souls of the son is mine: the soul that sinneth, it shall die" (Ez. 18:2-4). It is a rupture between two moralities, and as important as the one that took place between the two Testaments, as Jean Bottéro aptly demonstrates in his studies of those two great Biblical texts that are also monuments of universal literature, the *Book of Job* and *Ecclesiastes*. In them, the two authors drew up an exhaustive inventory not just of all the sufferings of humanity, but of all the injustices that God tolerates on Earth, of which even the righteous and the saints are often the victims. Job and the author of *Ecclesiastes* concluded that God did not want to be understood, that He preferred not to be, that "one needed not to understand Him in order to praise Him," and that one could hope for nothing from Him without praising Him and without loving Him no matter what He did. Here we find the *credo quia absurdum* of Tertullian. In any case, the injunction was clear: You must submit to the Law. But what if the law itself is not clear? Jesus will be questioned on the same issue: "Master, who did sin, this man, or his parents, that he was born blind?" (John 9:2—The cure of one born blind).

This takes nothing away from the fact that we do not ask ourselves questions about the meaning of life and history after every flood here, every seismic shock there, every epidemic or every famine somewhere else. In short, Evil is thinkable when it comes to the six billion inhabitants of the planet. But when it involves the fifteen million Jews in the world and the five million Israelis, then we ask ourselves questions about the mystery of existence, the presence of God, the monotheist revolution, and the fate of the Jews. That in any case is how the problem is experienced for the entire Western and, as a (negative) consequence, for the Arab and, often, African world.

the Jewish Prison
Jean Daniel

Rejection of
Fatality

Since I'm using these introductory observations to make, if not a premise, at least a foundation and launching pad for my thinking, I should linger over their reliability. Far from being the fruit of Judeocentric obsessions, they are on the contrary, I would like to point out, the outcome of a wish for liberation. I started with the idea that it was not desirable, or sound, or just, to brandish endlessly the argument of the "Jewish mystery," to sum up the problems of the world by the fact that we cannot reply rationally to questions posed by the singularity of the history of the Jews, the perpetuity of their journey, and the universality of their message.

Starting from this supposition, I undertook to be attentive to the way in which the Jews were living their new destiny after 1948. Obviously my conclusions were influenced by the birth and flourishing of the little Jewish State, which had become a military power in the shadow of the American superpower in order to face a hostile environment.

I was forced to realize that, born as it was in order to escape from Christian anti-Semitism, the State of Israel was developing and feeding a new Arab anti-Semitism. Powerful Jewish organizations and certain respectable intellectuals were eager to declare that it was a question of the resurgence of the same old phenomenon in a different land. A fatal conclusion. Unfaithful, in my opinion, to the message of Auschwitz, they do not recognize the distinction between the barbarities of which they had been the victims simply because they were born and because they existed, and on the other hand the vicissitudes they encounter because of what they do, on their own and of their own free will. For the first time in two thousand years, the Israelis are masters of their national fate. They are now in the domain of *doing* and no longer just in that of *being*. But now some of them, forever darkened by the fatality of Evil, reveal themselves to be incapable of distinguishing between the disasters they underwent in Auschwitz and the wars they are waging in Israel, on an even playing field with their enemies. This feeling of the fatality of an eternal and omnipresent anti-Semitism began to confirm me in the idea that there was indeed something that resembled, in the Jewish mystery, a prison.

Here, I should warn the reader that I will oscillate constantly, and sometimes even without caring about seeming balanced, between examining initiatives attributed to men and those that are supposed to translate the will of God. In other words, for my purposes it makes no difference whether one expresses oneself as if one were a believer, or tries to be an unbeliever.

What Transcendence?

To tell the truth, and to prolong this precautionary digression, it is best for me to state clearly right away that I have adopted, on the subject of these questions, an anachronistic attitude inherited from Ernest Renan, revitalized and revived by Jean Bottéro. I think there is something divine in the undertakings of those who have imagined God, but that in itself is not enough to establish the existence of God. I think some of the successive editors of the main texts of the Bible, as remote as they might be from history and sometimes from legend itself, attained a sublimity that has a whiff of transcendence. In a word, human imagination and art have continually invited humanity to a kind of transcendence, even though humans end up not freeing themselves from the mesh of a net they have patiently and brilliantly woven, the sovereign perversity of which they attribute to the wrath of God. In the end, and as we will see further on, there are no more unbelievers. There are believers who know they believe and who assume it, and there are unbelievers who act, without assuming it, like believers. That's another story, but we will keep finding it scattered throughout these pages.

What have the inheritors of Judaism done? We should note that the most disparate historians agree that there have been quite distinct moments on the path towards the formation of what we call today Jewish thought. And that Paul, when he decreed that there was no need to be Jewish in order to be faithful to the message of Judaism, tried to break the few remaining restrictions he had strengthened while he still called himself Saul of Tarsus. And in Christianity, the behavior that was decided on during the early councils and applied by the Church from the Crusades till the Inquisition was quick to close certain windows that had been opened in the Gospels. We find, then, a prison no doubt, but of quite a different kind. Finally, it is obvious that Islam has a conquering and global mission that aims to impose itself on the faithful of all humanity both present and future, or as Jacques Berque says, to invite them to a voluntary servitude and to a *marveling submission*.

The fact nonetheless remains that it is Judaism that invented the single god. It is from His message or His revelations that a doctrine was spread according to which one is damned by fleeing from the missions associated with being Chosen, from the Covenant, from settling in a Judaicized land. Not only does God grant the Jews a land already inhabited by a people that in principle is as dear to Him as any other, but He commands the newcomers, who are the newly chosen, to battle the natives; and He condemns them to act in the conquered country in an exemplary way, that is to say without worshipping the Canaanite gods and without forgetting the Torah or the Ten Commandments. When we see the level of demands, even of caprice, that God manifests with regard to His People, we indeed have to remind ourselves that these are the Jews who, in successive strokes, invented this god for themselves, and that this invention took on an autonomous existence, independent of its inventors. As a Jewish psychoanalyst said, there is often a sadomasochistic relationship between the created God and the people, His creator.

In any case, the present essay will revolve around these themes. In a certain sense, it is a form of testimony. It is in effect nothing but a testimonial. To follow the advice of the historian Marc Bloch, I have to return to the witness that I am. And, first of all, to the Jew that I was.

I.
the Witness

Naked came I out of my mother's womb,
and naked shall I return thither.

Job 1:21.

Inside. Outside.
Suspicion

I have the keenest respect for people like Robert Badinter, Daniel Barenboim, Ady Steg, Pierre Vidal-Naquet, and other friends who are exemplary Jews but who do not need to be Jewish to be exemplary. We don't ask ourselves the prison question when we look at them. They might indeed be in the prison, but they act as if it doesn't exist. To a different degree (and in the past), the same was true for Freud and Einstein, as violently opposed as they might have been to Zionism. Both called themselves atheist Jews (and Freud wanted to be *heretical*). But after Nazism they "enlisted," as they say in the army. No one at that time would have dreamt of saying to either of them that he was "outside the Community." That, however, is what Théo Klein, an admirably broad-minded man, an affirmed but open-minded Jew, said about me. At least, that is what he suggests the Community thinks of me. "Outside"? Is he, then, an opponent *from within*? That is not how I have steadily, in all my books, referred to my own Jewish family. Yet after all, there must be something true in the

impression I make. Formed in my youth by André Gide, I
have always detested closed milieus. I have always wanted
to go see what was behind the walls. At home, in my large
house, one could breathe; outside, in the *street of the Jews*,
no. As I grew older, it was only aesthetics and emotions
that ever made me feel separate from other people. Later I
will return to what attracted me to other religions by way of
these motivations. Finally, to say things simply, my feeling
of spontaneous, visceral belonging expresses a
Mediterranean Frenchness of which Judaism is only one
component. Often since then I have declared myself a "Jew
from solidarity." I do so again and emphasize that this
solidarity is unfailing. What I can describe *from outside*,
on the other hand, is all the community manifestations of
Jews grouped into tribes; it is difficult for me not to see in
them communitarian aspects that distress me. In any case,
the essential thing is to find out whether, thanks to this
outsider stance, I am or am not led to relevance.

It was when I was exercising my profession as a historian
that I had the experience of what Sartre called "imprisonment in identity structures." For Sartre, the philosopher of
freedom, it was a question of rejecting the reduction of a
man to his decisions. Sartre on the contrary preferred to
judge a man by the way in which he surpassed them. It is
in this spirit, that of the threat of confinement, that I experienced the pressures I constantly encountered, pressures
to be more specific about the way in which I was living

my Judaism. Some Jewish figures, and even a few close friends, were concerned about seeing me, according to them, "objectivizing" (that was the jargon of the time) my adherences. According to them, I was speaking of Jewishness as if it were something external.

Whether it was my political writings or my biographical writings, they claimed that my digressions on the Israeli-Arab conflict and my recourse to childhood memories had served as alibis for me to avoid fully assuming my "Jewishness." But I myself tended to think that I had already said a lot about this "problem" and that people in general were prone to speak of it too much. But such is the court of public opinion, and such is the dogma, that an assertion like mine, which detected in that excess a certain complacency, immediately appeared suspect to them. Since I thought the Jewish Question was talked about too much, they took my silence as my secret preference for dissimulation. And didn't that make me one of those who, shamefully, of course, yearn for that fatal assimilation, which throughout the centuries has only ended by surprising, catching unawares, disarming the victims, forever marked, of persecution? This is a question that is thought to be very modern, in the form in which our young people ask it today and try to impose it: In other words, suspecting that persecution has something to do with how the Jews behave, and not crediting that anti-Semitism is a basic category of mind—that, to them, is already a betrayal.

the Jewish Prison
Jean Daniel

Self-Hatred or
Captive Mind?

I have always been irritated by the interpretations of the unconscious content in suggestions that one formulates. These interpretations are to found in the various "suspicion" theories. This is the attitude of psychoanalysts, Marxists, linguists, ethnologists—in short, all those who, believing in predetermination, suppress in the end all freedom of thought and expression, all responsibility for what one expresses. We speak, but it's a *that* (or an "it") that speaks in our place, and we do not know what we mean, or what we say signifies. Our statements are supposed to reveal something completely different from what they express. To be specific, my entire discourse on Jewishness must only betray an attitude about the Jews that I am hiding from myself. In this case, there is no longer any way to conduct an argument or to carry out the least analysis. We are objects of study and not thinking subjects.

No doubt, when great anthropologists evoked so-called primitive mentality or so-called savage thought, their mission was to describe myths and to discover, in the case of Lévi-Strauss, that famous "structural unconscious," which has remained invisible and unexpressed. But the tribes studied do not themselves claim to rationalize their thoughts. They leave that to the anthropologists. Now, however, we are seeing more and more disciplines arising that attribute to modern societies a hidden discourse, the meaning of which only the great priests can grasp and decipher.

Here we are not far from this "captive mind" that Milosz so
admirably described in thinking about the Bolshevik
exploitation of Marxist theology. This observation, already
made in several domains, is particularly timely when it is a
question of reflecting on monotheist religions and, perhaps,
particularly on Judaism. Even before one expresses oneself,
and the very instant when one does express oneself, the
question that haunts the interlocutor is to know how much
one is tempted (by a diversion that can only be a suspicious
alibi) to emerge more or less from orthodoxy. It is no longer
a question of an exchange of thoughts, but of a project of
detecting the bad reasons because of which one is supposedly trying to distance oneself somehow from Judaism. To
judge all these reasons, the spiritual advisors play the pros-
ecutors. They lie in wait for the moment when they can
make their diagnosis: The confessor is no doubt the victim
of the notorious "self-hatred." I will not linger over the origin or evolution of this concept, which is far from concerning only Jews. How else can one characterize the pages that
one of the founders of sociology, the Algerian-Tunisian
Arab Ibn Khaldun, devoted in the Fourteenth Century to
his clan, his tribe, his family, his people? As to modern
times and France, one could say that no one has ever so
hated in himself his own Romanian-ness as did the
Romanian Emil Michel Cioran. The obsession of American
Blacks, so much have they internalized their being hated,

has been to make themselves white in order to be accepted by their enemies. But it is true that, with the Jews, a German Protestant writer, G. E. Lessing, knew, in the Eighteenth Century, in his play *Nathan the Wise*, how to spot subtly masochistic manifestations. "Self-hatred" implies that one justifies persecution by deeming oneself inferior to the persecutors. All those who have been colonized, who have been out of work, women sometimes, homosexuals often, have at some point undergone this test. The fact remains that the accusation of "self-hatred" remains the last recourse in denouncing a renegade among all those who refuse the ghettoization of intelligence.

An Impossible Singularity

This is the first instant when an open-minded person, or someone who claims to have an open mind, can have the feeling of a prison. He discovers the idea that you can escape from Jewishness only by betraying and denying *yourself*. You are given all the reasons for your incarceration. You are a prisoner precisely because you thought it possible not to be one. That, moreover, is a specificity: Even if you leave religion, you never leave the Jewish people and its unique destiny, even if, and sometimes especially if, you claim to be an unbeliever. To refuse the creator is not, cannot be, to refuse His creation and His creatures. You are condemned to belonging. And why does this condemnation exclude any choice? That is the most important thing of all. It is because, at bottom, there was no choice. At the outset, God suppressed choice because He imposed the Election. That is a paradox at once fascinating, wonderful, and tragic, this condemnation to the Good that suppresses a part of freedom. One can distance oneself from it only by practicing Evil or by leaving the people of God. It is a predestination without mercy. But being Chosen is not the only reason. In a different way, both the Shoah and Israel now present the same essential, eternal, and, in short, absolute quality. And these three qualifiers constitute, if you like, the invisible walls of the prison of the Jews.

I am starting from the hypothesis according to which God could have given the people He chose for Himself a doubly ambiguous message. Not only, insofar as one can impute an aim to God, did He impose on the Jews, notably through the intermediary of Moses and after the Covenant concluded with Abraham, the obligation to obey the Ten Commandments that only saints could truly obey. In fact only the chosen one, which for me is another name for a saint, can claim to satisfy such requirements. But there is more: By forbidding the chosen ones to be saints, God gives every freedom to the Devil to hound them. He keeps the Shoah shrouded in enigma. He does not explain it. He absents Himself. Or He laughs. What is more, He does not provide a formula that can reconcile this requirement of holiness with which "priests and witnesses" should be invested, with the promise (which has become a reality after two thousand years) of a territorial existence within a State—a material, temporal institution, implying state secrets, reasons of state, state interests, the formation of soldiers and warriors, that leads to the invoking of a nationalism of the individual that thus betrays the universality of the commandments. Isn't there, in the end, a paradox in asking a people to be "exemplary" while knowing that this exemplarity can be only a privilege of God? Isn't there, besides, a cruel contradiction between granting Israel a land confiscated from others and the requirement for a national holiness?

I do not hesitate to add to these assertions a very subjective dimension. I could never accept the idea that there is a definitive determination and that it compels one to adherence. What I find most exciting in the definitions I find of secularity is that this concept, the fruit of long conquests, confers on the State the function of protecting the individual from the group. From this point of view, I cannot accept the idea that there is a Jewish determination, that this determination is divine, and that one cannot escape from it. Against such a concept, my whole being revolts. But it is with at least as great a firmness that I refuse any indifference with respect to the persecutions inflicted on the Jewish people, an indifference that might be suspected because I do not grant this suffering a dimension of trans-rationality or transcendence. That leads to immersing oneself in solidarity with the suffering Jews when they suffer, even if only to prove, to prove to *oneself*, one's freedom. This solidarity, free of any determination, flourishes in the universal and makes all peoples more interdependent.

The Paternal Legacy   My refusal stems not just from the chance occurrences of personal experience, even if these occurrences have fed my awareness of it. I like to talk about how much, with us, religion was a family matter, not a community one, and to what point my father was its only high priest. I also like to tell about how much I was marked by the heroic tale, told by my brother, of how our father took action by answering racist insult with force. A decisive story insofar as it distanced and even excluded in advance the figure of the Jew as a moaning, humiliated, submissive, passive being.

The tribal structures of our large family welcomed and integrated elements foreign to our religion without dissolving them and without arousing any major disruptions. Thus in the course of the same week I sometimes attended the circumcision of a newborn and the First Communion of a Catholic child. An entire, very mixed, family can meet each other without the least surprise in either a church, or a temple, or a synagogue to celebrate a rite in accordance with the beliefs of a given parent. No one ever felt betrayed or blasphemed, and, among those who are the most careful to respect the memory of their Jewish grandfather, there are young people raised in the Christian faith and who intend to observe its commandments.

I admit that all this can seem unusual and, in any case, hardly representative. I will emphasize, with those who lecture on the universality of the Jewish message in mind, that the august man who served as patriarch of our family, my father, succeeded rather well in this sense, even if his distant offspring invoke God in different places and with other languages. So I have never, as you will understand, felt the necessity to strengthen my Jewish soul in a ghetto where people barricade themselves against the baleful aggressions of assimilation.

On the contrary, we thought of ourselves, according to the words of Léon Blum, as sons of the Revolution and of the republican school. The Collège Colonial of Blida counted for a lot with me and, with its militant, progressive, rational secularity, it fought the neo-ritualistic, neo-mystical irrationality there could also be in the family. In short, I cried over the death of Socrates before I cried over Job.

Such an education for a long time led my generation, or at least a part of it, to see in the supposed act of being Chosen only a sign of infamy—a yellow star—that anti-Semites imposed on the Jews to separate them from humanity. And if some of our fathers intoned the wish of "next year in Jerusalem," they expressed nothing but a hope for a better life, either in this world, or in the other, in an indeterminate future. Moreover, I think it is of some consequence that the faithful, even today in the heart of the synagogues of Israel, have not suppressed from their prayers this promise of reunion in a year's time in this Jerusalem where they already are.

As a Sign of Opening Up

Without wanting to, then, and without realizing it, I took the path of what is called *assimilation*. In fact, this path had been very well traveled and marked out by my parents and my grandparents. They had taught me to detest everything that is closed in on itself, everything that excludes, everything that's retreating or withdrawn. At home, in the large house of my huge family, everything was welcoming and open. Of course, over the front door, there was a kind of religious talisman that recalled our Jewishness. But, to me, it didn't mean rejection of others. That sort of meaning existed in many houses other than our own. That is why modernist rabbis rise up against such a pagan practice of the sacred. But we will see, in the following anecdote, how a concept can lose in comprehension what it gains in extension.

A scholar of Jewish Law, recently invited onto a television program, explained the significance of the little cylinder (the *mezuzah*) placed at the front door of the house or of the parents' bedroom in many families, and which contains the words of God: "Hear, O Israel, the Lord our God, the Lord is one." One might think, then, that the owner of the house is enjoined to present himself, and permanently to come to terms with himself, as Jewish, and that, by doing this, he separates himself from whomever he welcomes.

By no means. Such an interpretation would mean rejection of the foreigner, and since many essential texts remind us that the Jewish people were first of all a people of foreigners, the exegete, in a way that was not contrived because of his erudition, emphasized that the *mezuzah* expressed the fact that God was at home in this house. That it's He who welcomes the house owner into the house just as the house owner should welcome all guests, whatever they might be, including those foreign to Judaism. This distinctive symbol should in principle identify, for the others, houses and individuals whose duty it is to welcome them.

This, however, is not what emerges from the studies that are conducted on all the rites, of dress or otherwise. The more the sign of belonging to Judaism is visible, the more the hard-core adherents of the faith try to demonstrate that it is a matter of believers chosen to defend universal values. One could imagine the skullcap of some and the side-curls of others being made into the equivalents of the armbands that indicate chaplains during wars and first-aid workers after accidents. I am intentionally pushing logic to the point of caricature, since these distinctive signs emphasize, especially in the eyes of others, a difference that is experienced as a foreignness.

Ghetto, In practice, moreover, in daily life, this ghettoizing
Aristocracy, attitude—usually the result of persecution—is not at all
and Fraternity perceived as an offer of fraternity. The uniform of the Salvation Army leaves no room for doubt: Only those whose sole objective is aid, solidarity, and charity wear it. This is not the case for those who want to be seen as different, either to live more intensely the tribal or religious and enthusiastic belonging to a community, or to flaunt a distinctive feature, and thus a separation.

In other words, in the most Christianizing interpretation of Judaism, the difference is offered as a sign of aristocracy in the ancient sense of the word, that is to say that it designates the best. The different one shouldn't be the strongest, or the most mysterious, or the most ambitious: His obligation is to be the best. He gives others the possibility of reminding him of it. On the subject of the veil of the Muslims, the great Arabic poet Adonis wrote definitive and wonderfully *free* things.

Often the Jew becomes indignant because he observes, in the words of the great actress Sarah Bernhardt, that "others wish us to be better than anyone else." The actress was forgetting that in fact this was the impossible fate of Judaism, and that it had somehow either to fulfill it or refuse it completely.

We arrive, with this example, at a new entrance to the doors of the famous prison. By wanting to be different, by accepting such as the supposed will of God, by finding fault with those who try to smooth away this difference, even if they do so for the noblest reasons, the Jew condemns himself to be the best everywhere. Here we find again this condemnation to holiness that, I think, summarizes the impossible wager of Judaism and—even more serious—the temptation to accept as legitimate the persecutions committed against those who did not succeed in behaving like saints.

Maurras and the Dead

In my childhood, there was a lot of talk about a Monarchist daily paper, the *Action française*, and the anti-Semitic campaigns of its director, Charles Maurras. Maurras urged his readers to visit the monuments to the dead in their cities to see how few were the names of Jews who "died for their country."

Of course, this was a racist imposture. On one hand, since the proportion of French Jews was extremely low, there could only be a limited number of names connected with them on all the monuments: What is more, in their unequal dispersion, they were concentrated in some provinces more than others. On the other hand, for a doctrinarian like Charles Maurras, sacrifice of life was the least that was required to ascend to Frenchness. Even that might not be enough. The proof is that our generals "consumed," as we know, many regiments of the Senegalese infantrymen, the *Tirailleurs*, or the Moroccan *Tabors* during the two World Wars without anyone feeling the immediate need, especially on the side of the extreme right, to proclaim that the Blacks and the Berbers were fully fledged French citizens.

But, whether it was at school or, afterwards, under Pétain, being surrounded by non-Jews, having for my friends Christians who were, as I was, victims of the legislations of Vichy, the specificity of persecution was not glaringly self-evident for me early on. That came later on, progressively. At first I knew nothing of the grave and atrocious persecutions the Jews experienced simply because they were Jewish. And I did not have parents who died in concentration camps. Finally, the fact of having fought in the war in the Leclerc division gave me a different approach.

As Claude Lanzmann's later film, *Sobibor*, shows, it is entirely different to die fighting than to die passively. Combat institutes an equality. If the enemies win, it's in the course of a fight. One can tell oneself then that it's not the Jew in us that they hit, but the combatant.

the Jewish Prison
Jean Daniel

A Patriotic
Lesson

This is the lesson I learned from José Aboulker, offspring of great Jewish doctors in Algeria, and himself the head of a neurobiology department, as well as a fighter in the Resistance. In 1942, I wanted to enlist and leave for Gibraltar, but he restrained me. He told me, "We have a mission here; there will be something to do." He knew about the impending American landing. I explained to him that I was in a hurry to fight, even if only to free myself from our predicament of being stripped of French nationality by the Vichy authorities. He laughed and asked me if I were a believer. No. Well, in that case, what makes sense, he advised me, is never to do anything that has to do with belonging to Judaism. "For my part, I make sure I do nothing whatsoever that is conditioned by my Jewishness. In the war, which we will join together, I myself will fight against the Nazis as a man, as a Frenchman, and of course as a Jew also. But I do not want to separate any of the three motivations." "If you die," I pointed out to him, "they will say that you fought only to defend the honor of the persecuted Jews." "Maybe, but I alone will know what I died for."

During this period when I was deprived of my nationality, I never for an instant felt the need to call into question my belonging to the French nation. It seemed so natural to me to be French that I couldn't conceive that a trick of the law could strip me of this ancient baptism. The way I define the ties that join me to France is close to the way in which the Ukrainian Jewish writer Yosef Hayim Brenner, who settled in Palestine in 1909, described his ties with the Jewish people: "We are Jewish by our actual, real-life experience, in our inmost depths. Without any intellectual definition, without any absolute axioms, without any dogmatic engagements.... The love of our people and of its moral qualities is one thing that is not necessary to recall. It is obvious that there is no cause to take great pride in being Jewish, just as one does not take great pride in loving daylight or the sun. We are patriots, fervent patriots. But our patriotism is not the kind for which we would do what our conscience would disdain." The fact remains that I could always break with France, whereas one is supposed never to be able to break with Judaism.

Assimilation or It is, I know, good form today to criticize assimilation. I
Emancipation? will not attempt here to retrace its history—that would be neither necessary nor timely for our project—but to discuss the dynamics of it.

The emancipation of the Jews by the French Revolution made the notion of a "people" null and void. From then on, there were only French citizens, of Jewish origin (or faith). All Jews could have said, as Hannah Arendt observes, "what Kafka said one day on the subject of his belonging to the Jewish people: 'My people, supposing I have one.'"

the Jewish Prison
Jean Daniel

The speech by Clermont-Tonnerre in the Constituent Assembly, on December 23, 1789, summarizes the whole doctrine of assimilation as it has long been triumphant in France: "We must refuse everything to the Jews as a nation and grant them everything as individuals. We must ignore their judges, since they must have ours; in the State they must not form a political body or an order. They must individually be citizens."

We should recall, as does Dominique Schnapper, that, until the Revolution, the Jews formed a special political body: "The Jewish communities before political modernity were entirely religious and political." The Jews were thus commanded to renounce their existence as a nationality with its particular laws, its judges, its tribunals. They had to accept the status of one simple religious community among others. That is precisely what Clermont-Tonnerre expresses when, as Robert Badinter points out in *Libres et Égaux* (Free and equal), he "wants emancipation to make everything that marks the difference of the Jews, everything that constitutes them as a community distinct from others—in a word, everything that makes them a 'nation'—disappear."

In the same way, by defining Judaism as a religion— the practice of which stems from the private sphere and reduces Jewish identity to a confession of faith—the Constituent Assembly settled the difficult debate (which was not yet a debate but which, because of these new demands, was about to become one) concerning the very essence of Jewishness. As Laurent Theis wrote: "This was responding authoritatively to a question that was in reality unsolvable: Is Jewish identity entirely and exclusively contained in the confession of faith?"

From Dreyfus
to Marc Bloch
The Dreyfus affair, paradoxically, would be the revealing indicator of the assimilation of the Jews with France. I often think back to what Levinas told me about his father, who said to him, "A country that completely tears itself apart, that divides itself, in order to save the honor of a little Jewish officer, is a country you should hurry to!" There are two version, then. For Herzl, the Dreyfus affair kindles the idea of a Jewish State, but for Levinas' father, it revives the wish to see in France a special place of welcome. The idea of integration was foreign to the Jewish peoples of Eastern Europe. The France of that time, ready to indict its army on the eve of a war (in 1914), had something thrilling about it. That's what I think a lot of intellectuals—like Zeev Sternhell and Bernard-Henri Lévy—miss when they condemn *French ideology*. The assimilation of the Jews into France was expressed in the most moving and profound way by Marc Bloch in *L'Étrange défaite* (Strange defeat). He is the one who would also articulate the most beautiful definitions of France.

the Jewish Prison
Jean Daniel

And (to begin at the end) I will recall that the majority of French citizens did not voluntarily rally round the measures taken in their name, rashly and eagerly, by the Vichy government. The studies by Serge Klarsfeld establish that the number of French people who saved Jews is considerable. Why? It is estimated that two French Jews out of three were saved from deportation, which means that 240,000 were saved. What does this imply, saving Jewish people? That the concierge consented to it, and the grocer too. Only one indiscretion, one leak, was enough to make the rescue operation fail. In short, for tens of thousands of Jews to be saved, the help of millions of French people was necessary. I do not think there was one anti-Semitic fatality in France.

Back from
the Camps

That said, could we retain this assimilationist attitude after Auschwitz? Could the answers that we gave before Nazism to the question "what kind of Jew are you?" be the same afterwards? It is impossible not to take the Shoah into account. But it is a matter of knowing how this rupture of civilization influences our personal lives. To reckon with the monstrous absurdity of the Shoah, many Jews have had recourse either to faith, or to the call for a "return to Zion," or to an attitude of shadowy mistrust with regard to France. I experienced none of these temptations.

In 1946, I discovered not just the existence of camps, or of concentration camps, but of *extermination* camps. How? The answer to this is important. I discovered the abomination of abominations from books written by non-Jews. First of all David Rousset, Robert Antelme, Louis Martin-Chauffier. Then Jorge Semprun. To the point that I no longer associate the universe of concentration camps, the tragedy of extermination, with Judaism. The term "Shoah," moreover, was not yet in use. But there is more. When I finally immersed myself in texts as essential as those by Margaret Buber Newman and David Grossman, the authors of which are Jewish indeed, then I learned that there was hardly any difference between a Bolshevik camp and a Nazi camp, and that one could emerge from one only to be interned in the other. And I am ready to accept that one can categorize them under the same term, as Hannah Arendt did, whose concept of *totalitarianism* evokes Bolshevism as well as Nazism. For myself, I had to wait for the books of Primo Levi, published very late in France, to understand how, in the end, one could speak legitimately of the uniqueness of the Shoah.

As the historian Jean-Pierre Azéma recalls, "No one, or almost no one, was interested in the 'Jewish question.' For Resistance fighters, for public opinion, one had to concern oneself with the totality of the victims—the prisoners, the deportees, Jewish or not, the victims of air raids, the

the Jewish Prison
Jean Daniel

tortured or executed Resistance fighters. They all deserved the same compassion, they all had the same dignity. A part of the Jewish community adapted this point of view. It did not want to set itself apart from the other victims. In the period preceding the war it had been only too distinct. Above all, outside of the Jewish community, few people had understood the philosophical and historical uniqueness of extermination. It was only after the trial of Eichmann in Jerusalem in 1961 and at the end of the 1970's that one began, with the publication of important texts, to see Vichy recast in the light of persecution of the Jews."

Back from the camps, the deportees did not want to speak. Of course, as Simone Weil told me personally, this silence was of the heaviest kind. Freed by the English in April 1945 after spending thirteen months in Birkenau, then in Bergen-Belsen, when she was still just eighteen years old, she had to resign herself, she said, to silence. "As soon as we returned, we tried to speak, to express ourselves," but no one really wanted to hear their words. "Indifference?" "Conspiracy of silence?" "Scorn for what we were saying?" "Too uncomfortable to hear?" A "mixture of all of that," she concluded.

But there is also the extraordinary case of Claude Lévi-Strauss. Very recently (in June 2003), the author of *Tristes Tropiques* confided in me the disarming ingenuousness that had inspired his expectations after the return of the deportees.

He himself could hardly believe it, but he confided in me that he had thought that after the genocide the Jewish problem would practically cease to exist. If he trusted his own feelings and those of the people close to him, a group of perfectly integrated (or assimilated, if you like) Jewish families, then the Jews would have only one single inclination, which would be to be resorbed into the community from which the barbarians had dissociated them. My mistake is very revealing, he said, about my ignorance of a wish for Jewish affirmation, but perhaps this wish would have been less intense without the birth of the State of Israel.

The Example of Jorge Semprun So the period of becoming aware and taking stock of the concentration camps came long after the Liberation, long after the end of the camps. The way in which that occurred set me keenly on alert. I understood the wish of Jewish people to say, "Since we have been persecuted, exterminated for what we are, we have to be even more what people think we are." But that offended me.

Daniel Bernstein, who, at the time of the Liberation, received authorization to publish a newspaper, *Caliban* (of which I eventually became the director) defended another position. He had joined the war as a Resistance fighter in the famous British "Buckmaster" network. All the members of this network were arrested, but only Bernstein was sent to Buchenwald. When he returned, he was decorated. Jewish organizations then tried to integrate him into their ranks, but he refused. I was quite young at the time and I told him of my admiration for what he had done. When I questioned him about his decision not to join the Jewish organizations, he replied: "I don't want to be separated yet again from my Resistance brothers. They forced me to, and I could do nothing about it. But if I chose to imitate them, I would be betraying my reasons for fighting in the first place." And he never joined anything but secular associations of Resistants and deportees.

At *Le Nouvel Observateur*, early on, there was a woman named Irène Allier, daughter of a great Jewish Resistance fighter, Georges Altman. She liked to recall a saying of her father's. Every time people talked to him about going back to the synagogue, about belonging to the community, or about making a defense in the name of the Jews, he would say, "Hitler didn't win the war! Why do you expect me, out of bravado, to conform to the idea Hitler had of us? It was not in the name of Jewish identity that we fought Nazism."

I also remember a scene that took place at the *Nouvel Observateur*. Jorge Semprun had come, at our invitation, to discuss his lastest book, *Quel beau dimanche!* (What a beautiful Sunday), which we all admired. But, in the course of the discussion, he did not dismiss the idea that the Stalinist concentration camps might have been as horrible and as deadly as Hitler's camps. Despite Semprun's authority, based on his experience which we were grateful to him for expressing, he had disturbed our little group. There were some for whom the equivalence of the camps risked implying an equivalence of regimes. No matter how anti-Stalinist they were, they refused the ideological pitfalls of such an assertion. Others stated that Hitlerism had been conceived as a doctrine of racial supremacy and as an ethnic imperialism, whereas Communism, even including its Stalinist form, belonged to the tradition of the great egalitarian dreams of humanity. But the unhappiest of us all was a young Jewish sociologist whose parents had been exterminated by the Nazis and who feared that the statements of a man as beyond reproach as Semprun might be exploited to reinforce the argument of the banality of evil.

Might the preparation, organization, and realization of the Nazi monstrosity have equivalents elsewhere? Can the will to exterminate an entire people, not just any people, but the Jewish people, because of its difference, because of its origin, its history and its mission—can this intention be compared to any others? Questions like that were surely what made our friend suffer.

the Jewish Prison
Jean Daniel

Sartrean
Liberation

Far from the idea of being Chosen, cut off from my Jewish sources since the death of my father, and preserving only the rites that recalled my childhood, I became, quite naturally, a Jew defined by anti-Semitism. And when Sartre published his *Reflections on the Jewish Question,* I felt that he had written it for me. The arguments of this book are regarded today as a disgraceful, sometimes even suspicious, oversimplification. But while it is possible that they don't cover the breadth of what defines Jewishness in its origins and its horizons, it is a fact that the arguments defended in his essay have liberated an entire generation of Jews.

At the time, our reading of Sartre was a great relief. Why does Sartre liberate? First of all, if he liberates, it's because there are a lot of chains. He frees us from being locked up in a prison whose bars are made of the decree of a fatality of inheritance and behavior. According to this destiny, you cannot not be Jewish if you are or if you have been, or if your parents and the parents of your parents have been Jewish. The idea is thus imposed that, as soon as you enter the world as a Jew, you struggle in vain; you will never manage to free yourself or reclaim the innocence of freedom. Freedom is no longer innocent. But Sartre maintains that Jewishness is nothing but the product of the gaze of the anti-Semite. In fact, without the gaze of the other, the Jew would not feel Jewish and would not worry about so being. The prison is no longer constructed by

God, even as a blessing. It is constructed by the enemy. There are no more bars to cherish or chains to bless.

Suddenly Sartre's interpretation gives the anti-Semite a considerable importance. Being does not inhere in the Jew. Being inheres in the executioner. It is in the gaze. For the Jew a kind of hollowness, if not non-existence, is reserved. Hence the reaction, confronted by this vertigo of nothingness, of some Jews who are aware that they exist apart from this gaze. These first reactions—which accused Sartre of emptying Judaism of all its positivity, of all its content, of all its richness—constitute, especially since the Shoah, an additional proof of my interpretation: The Jews do not see any universe outside of their prison.

From Mendès France to Ben-Gurion

When I read Sartre's essay, this feeling of deliverance from myself urged me towards freedom, to choice in other words, towards political involvement and actions in accord with my own nature. By this release, an individual is born who is freed from the group, from a community, from a race. The instant your identity is reduced to the gaze of the enemy, there is suddenly an enemy who makes you free. In Sartre's concept—and this is why I am one of its last defenders, against even Sartre himself, since Benny Lévy made him correct and renounce his statements in his final moments—is the idea that the enemy is so much the creator of the prison that you have only to rise up against him to get out of it. (In his introduction to Frantz Fanon's *The Wretched of the Earth*, Sartre went even further). And, in that instant, Sartre gave the Jew the definition of his freedom. Sartre showed in stark relief the idea of the prison of the Jews, and he opened the prison. Everyone would try to close it up again afterwards, but it's thanks to Sartre that I discovered the prison, as well as the possibility of escaping from it.

I recall Pierre Mendès France who, to the question "What does your Judaism consist of?" replied: "I was born Jewish, anti-Semites think of me as Jewish, and my children know they are Jewish." These statements are instructive in that they confirm the pertinence of Sartre's intuition, but also in that they emphasize that one can extract a choice from them. What, in short, is Mendès France saying? "I was born Jewish, but," he says in an interview in a Jewish journal, "I'm not going to say, in order to win you over, that my Judaism is more than an inheritance. I am labeled by the gaze of others. At the same time, it is true that this gaze is transmitted, since my children know they are Jewish, yet without that fact bringing them a faith or a practice."

And for him, for me, and for so many others, even less did this condition of birth imply reassembling in the Promised Land consecrated in 1948 by the establishment of the Hebrew State.

Along this line, one cannot avoid confronting Israel too, along with its mystical-temporal epic. A country, a nation, a State, a people founded wholly on the Book. And what a Book! The first time I met Ben-Gurion, since he was talking to me about Spinoza whom he liked despite everything, I asked him if he believed in God. The question did not shock him, but he replied that it was not an "Israeli" question. For him, one of the founders of the Hebrew State, and its Prime Minister when I asked him the question, it was enough to "believe in the Book."

He had it on his table, that Book. And he said he used it for everything and anything. Can religion be separated from the Revelation? How can such an importance be attributed to a text if it is not based on something transcendental? Ben-Gurion replied that it was not a question of denying the transcendence behind the text, but of evading a definition of it. In any case, there was a Book that contained the main principle of humans and the world. That was enough to found a State and a destiny. The interview, alas, did not continue.

When it comes to that famous Book, it is true that it contains everything, that is to say, it contains a history that is wholly human, with violence, crime, wars. Stories in which the chosen people, in order to survive as an instrument of divine will, are compelled to inflict the worst calamities on its enemies—and with the aid of God. The ten plagues of Egypt: Are these the works of heroes and saints? When Israel anticipates an attack, wins its war, and occupies territories in order to prevent another attack, then

the Jewish Prison
Jean Daniel

refuses to return those territories by invoking the Bible and the true enough fact that, in the Book, the occupied territories are called "Judea" and "Samaria"—in this case, how is the Hebrew State behaving? Like any other State? Like the land where, after centuries of wandering and suffering, the chosen people gathers together for a time? Can it aspire to both behaviors at once, and in that case, ask other nations for two kinds of understanding or cooperation?

This is not just the famous mystical ambiguity of the Jewish fate, the identical and the different, the particular and the universal, wandering and taking root. This is the whole problem of Evil that is being posited. And of violence. If there are problems that a chosen people must resolve, shouldn't those take precedence?

The justification of the Israeli presence in Palestine comes first of all from the transcendence evoked in the Book; then from the memory of the territory where the epic of this Book unfolded; and finally from the confirmation of Election by one of the most atrocious and most apocalyptic manifestations of divine wrath, the genocide. But even then one cannot avoid questioning, from a faithfully Jewish point of view—I would even say, from within its most rigorous orthodoxy—the legitimacy of the methods of combat used by Israel.

The Republic and Communitarianism

Let us resume the thread of our narrative. When, in 1967, de Gaulle described the Jews as "an elite people, sure of itself and domineering," I did not react in the same way as, for instance, Raymond Aron did. What offended the many Jews who, like me, were working at his side, was his use of the term "people," in the singular. For men like Joseph Kessel, Romain Gary, Georges Boris, and Léo Hamon, who joined him very soon after the summons of June 18, the people to which they thought they belonged was the French people. That de Gaulle distinguished them from his companions—that is what shocked them and me. I thought de Gaulle, who had been surrounded by French Jews in the Resistance, did not have the right to enclose French Jews in an unconditional belonging to the State of Israel.

It was the legacy of the French Revolution he seemed to be calling into question again. After Vichy, despite Vichy, and against all those Jews who were beginning to question the French model of assimilation, we held our membership in the French nation as prime, unquestionable, and irreversible. As good heirs of the Revolution, a national or political concept of the "Jewish people" seemed to us absolutely foreign. Even if, of course, in the private sphere, one might choose to remain faithful to Judaism.

It made a crack in the heart of the Republic at the very moment when the arrival in France of the Sephardic Jews from North Africa, distinguished by a multi-secular piety but also by a communal anxiety, would precipitate a

the Jewish Prison
Jean Daniel

feeling of communitarianism. A feeling that has only increased since then, and with which I cannot empathize.

Alterities   Since those days, hasn't there been a general return to faith, obedient to a movement around me at which I was present? No. I should say that, as an active anti-colonialist—that is the path by which I entered politics—I was very quickly put into contact with Islam. And since rehabilitating Islam was at bottom to contribute to decolonization, I felt the temptation, often described by ethnologists, to take on its values and beliefs. I was wounded in Bizerte and I shared the lives of Tunisians. Intense memory of tenderness. But I remained outside its faith. In Algeria and in Morocco I had ties of affection that would leave traces in me. To pursue the question of religion, I should observe that from the moment that the Catholic Church put into effect its *aggiornamento*, that's to say starting with John XXIII, during the relinquishment of its anti-Judaism, and then its formal apology to the Jews, I felt free to admire what I had always secretly admired—namely the Christian adventure. I use the term "adventure" deliberately, for there is no faith. But I gathered a lot of information about the first century, which, I think, is one of the most exciting times in history. Prophets kept arising, but there was only one who fully appeared, according to Renan's analysis in his *Life of Jesus*: Christ.

In my childhood, I encountered this hero neither on the face of the curate of our church, nor on the faces of the parishioners who crowded into the bakeries at noon on Sunday after Mass and who evinced rejection, exclusion, closed-mindedness, fear, and scorn. Christians for us were anti-Semitic officers, and their wives, petty-bourgeois snobs. I do not remember having felt the slightest tinge of spirituality in their milieu. On the other hand, we had a history and geography teacher who, every week, introduced us to a great painter. And when the subject portrayed scenes of the Passion or the Ascension, he found, in order to praise the artists, words that I can say spoke to our souls. That is how, thanks to a very anti-clerical layperson and Secretary of the Socialist branch, I was moved for the first time by the face of Christ or the Virgin. I remember a painting, Leonardo da Vinci's *The Virgin and Saint Anne*, that struck me all the more since the Virgin's mother, about whom no one ever dares to say that she is Christ's grandmother, had a hairstyle and face that reminded me of a portrait of my own grandmother that we were used to seeing in a painting in our parents' bedroom. Da Vinci makes us experience all the degrees and all the emotions of maternal protection. Saint Anne was protecting Mary, who was protecting Christ. I had never experienced so deeply the warm and instinctive singularity of the maternal offering. A few years later, though, a friend—

the Jewish Prison
Jean Daniel

Jean Pelégri—with whom I shared a desk in elementary school had me read a poem by Paul Claudel, "La Vierge à midi" (The Virgin at noon).

> *It is noon. I see the church is open. I have to go in.*
> *Mother of Jesus Christ, I am not coming to pray.*
> *I have nothing to offer and nothing to ask.*
> *I am only coming, Mother, to look at you.*
> *To look at you, to cry out of happiness, to know that*
> *I am your son and that you are there.*
> *Just for an instant while everything stops.*
> *Noon!*
> *To be with you, Mary, in this place where you are.*
> *Not to say anything, just look at your face,*
> *To let my heart sing in its own language.*
> *Not to say anything, but just to sing because my*
> *heart is overfull,*
> *Like the blackbird who follows his idea in those*
> *spaces of sudden verse.*

I was not at all aware that such a poem expressing such sentiments could separate me from my own, and even from the best qualities that existed in my own feelings. It seemed to me that I myself was saying to my grandmother, that is to Anne, wife of Joachim and mother of Mary, that I was coming to see her only to look at her. Anne, mother of the mother of Jesus Christ whom da Vinci sublimated as emblematic, archetypical, the incarnate quintessence of protective compassion. I went about my business, but this memory left traces in me. It gave me the idea that one had to look there, on that side, to grasp the faithful expression of my Jewish family.

As you can see, in da Vinci's masterpiece, the future Christ, the infant Jesus, did not at the time interest me at all. He is, moreover, always more or less ridiculous in the greatest masterpieces of the Italian or Flemish paintings I venerate. I do not know if a painter has ever tried to give him a personality other than that of an inane doll, but one, of course, protected, super-protected by the mother, the grandmother, the saints, the evangelists, the adorers. You have to look at everyone else to see what the infant will become and what is not yet... far from it. In this period of communitarianisms, I am aware that I am blaspheming, but that saves me from being too close to Christians in the present essay, for, when I come to the matter of cathedrals, I continue to be stunned, and I dream of cloisters and of all the ambulatories where we can gather to be ourselves while grandmothers watch over us.

The fact remains that Jesus would go on to say many things to get out of the prison of his father, his ancestors, his lineage, and his filiation. He would increase the number of chosen people, but he would ask them for a little more—for instance, to show the other cheek when they were slapped. Another servitude. Another prison. Another condemnation to holiness. But, by dying on the Cross, he would first of all condemn people to suffering. Before saving them, he would show them the path of martyrdom. All these Jews are sinners, just as they were before the Flood, or before the destruction of the temples, or before the deportation to Babylon. But where was Christ, grandson of Saint Anne, while his grandmother was dying in the concentration camps? Where was Mary during Auschwitz? I said it in my introduction. What does it matter to us, if we have to suffer, if God and his son suffer like us! But let us return to our dear prison.

The Rodinson Case

There is a man who has sometimes exasperated, sometimes fascinated, but always interested me: the Islamologist, Arabic scholar, and Orientalist Maxime Rodinson. He is Jewish; his parents were Communist Jews (so he was raised as an atheist) who died in the camps. He is, along with Jean-Pierre Vernant and others, one of the leaders of the Union Rationaliste. He is a scholar, and a specialist in all eastern languages. He will categorically deny that there is a Jewish specificity. For him, there is no such thing as Jewish nature, just an ill-fated, perverse culture. The Orientalist he is, the scholar he is, can prove whenever you like that there is no Jewish *mystery*. There have been civilizations that have disappeared and returned; there have been peoples who have been persecuted for a long time. This people *miraculously* survived only because it was prolonged by Christianity. Rodinson would go so far as to say that, without Christianity, Judaism would have collapsed like so many other ideologies. He pushes historical reasoning to its extreme logic.

But we can see very clearly that two things lead him to such a conclusion. First of all, he has a scholar's experience; secondly, Marxism has remained present in his work, even after his rejection of Communism.

This anthropologist and linguist has always struck me by the vastness of his knowledge and by the calm courage with which he wrote his life of Mohammed (*Mahomet*), a great classic. This man has always made me reflect, because I found it somewhat disconcerting that he didn't grant the death of his parents some immense incomprehensibility built of scandal and pain. He told himself instead that his parents had been victims of a simple barbarism, like other barbarisms. There is more than banalization in that; there is a historic normalization of suffering, of the concentration camps. According to Rodinson, horror is just a matter of varying degrees, according to the times. The proof of this, he observes, is that the Jews themselves talk of Babylon, of the first Temple, of Massada. There are always precedents.

I point out to him that his parents died in Auschwitz and that they were arrested as Jews. He replies: "No, they were arrested as Communists." When one reminds him that mainly Jews were deported to Auschwitz, he retorts that it was a question of chance. In his view, the will of Jewish culture to assert itself, to constitute itself as a separate civilization, insured the continuity of the Jewish people, but at the same time aroused rejection. He imputes a share of responsibility to the Jews themselves in this fate that was reserved for them. This is the opposite of Sartre. The main question is to know if, when the Jews say they are not men like other men, it is the others that make them different, or if they are the ones who want to be different and who insist so much on this difference that they provoke estrangements and separations, or else persecutions. It is in this give-and-take that Rodinson takes sides when he says that there is no reason to declare, in the name of History, that the Jewish people has a special fate. His attitude has never satisfied me.

Dissidence

Should we then classify Rodinson, against his will, among the dissidents? I call "Jewish dissidence" that tradition or lineage that extends from Flavius Josephus to Bruno Kreisky and includes Spinoza, Heinrich Heine, Simone Weil, Henri Bergson, Hannah Arendt, Edith Stein, and Edmond Husserl. We'll leave it to fanatics to baptize them as renegades. And to the maximalists the option of seeing in them the most banal manifestation of a very Jewish tradition. This latter interpretation, as we have seen, is quite widespread among the creators of systems; it consists in interpreting refusal above all. If you are not sick, the psychoanalyst will say that you have a health neurosis. Thus the Orthodox Jew, and historian, will see in the refusal to accept the concept of being Chosen, for instance, the proof of an indisputable and profound belonging to the chosen people. That is what happened to Spinoza in the seventeenth century.

I grew interested in a book by Alain Minc on Spinoza because the author used his hero to discover what a Jew could become without taking on Judaism, and especially without taking on belief. I then read and re-read Spinoza. With difficulty. With passion. And I came to the conclusion that Spinoza was not a "bad Jew." He was simply not a Jew at all. We would have to go back to a rehabilitative concept of marginality to make him a good Jew in the eyes of the prison jailers. The bad Jew, the marginal—the one who lives outside institutions, who does not behave in accord with Judaism—is still part of Judaism; he is an essential component of Judaism. I felt concerned. In Spinoza, was Minc concerned only with recovering the Jew? If one succeeds in perceiving a component of Judaism at a distance from Judaism, then one reveals that the bars of the prison can be invisible.

Let me call these marginal Jews dissidents, then. This will be my own way of showing my solidarity with them. For a dissident is neither indifferent nor alien to orthodoxy. He separates himself from it but he refers to it, and his dissidence would have little meaning without the orthodox reference he questions.

Like Spinoza, though, I cannot manage to believe truly, completely, that the Jewish people, despite the miracle of its continuity, is the unique witness of humanity, or the only instrument of divinity. And when, by chance, led on by the lyricism of the great Jewish or Christian texts, from Isaiah to Claudel, from Maimonides to Saint John of the Cross, I let myself be persuaded that the role of the Jewish people is at once predestined and privileged—even so I do not accept that it is alone in being so. Above all, I refuse to allow it to behave as if, under the grounds that it will be persecuted no matter what it does, it can permit itself to do whatever it pleases, for good or evil. As if, in the name of its Election—or of its curse—it could allow itself a different morality from that of other people.

Thus, in the heart of the prison of the Jews, it is indeed the concept of Election that we encounter first.

II.
Election

Only do not two *things* unto me: then will I
not hide myself from thee.
Withdraw thine hand far from me: and let
not thy dread make me afraid.

Job 13:20-21.

I am not a theologian or a historian of religions, nor do I mean to pose as one. I know only a little Latin, scarcely more Greek, and no Hebrew. My thoughts on the subject intend mainly to be those of a witness, a man who has taken part in History, in the events of his time, and who questions himself, not on the degree of fidelity that the believers—in this case the Jews—do or don't display, with respect to the sacred texts, but on the way in which they live their religion. And my main question, since everything depends on it, is this: How does the chosen people live its fact of being Chosen?

My aim is to demonstrate that this Election quickly proves to be impossible to endure, unless it is understood as the flip side of a curse. I have observed, in the course of my reading, that this Chosen notion embarrasses Jewish thinkers, who themselves continue, almost obsessively, to redefine it. Why, when, how does an individual, a group, a people, come to believe they are "chosen"? Whence come the idea of Election and the expression the "chosen people"? Scholars, often eminent Jews, keep "revisiting" the notion. Fewer are those who say, "That is how it is." Election, they assert, is not what you think—we no longer know what it is. Being Chosen is not being Chosen, and everyone gives a definition of Election fashioned from an insipid generosity that ends up emptying the specificity of the Judaic message of all its content.

The more theological ones among them relentlessly try to prove that it is not in any way a question of a privilege but of a "yoke," in no way a prerogative but a responsibility that the whole world shares. How do the Jews, and following them all the other peoples who believe they are chosen, reinterpret the multiple meanings of such an ambiguous message? How do they accommodate an injunction that surpasses the capabilities of the modern city-dweller?

Of course one can reply that the commandments, the injunctions, the directives, and messages set a standard of ideals for all moralities and all religions, and that these ideals cannot be expected to be easily attained, or even ever attained. We can keep this objection in mind from the outset and allow that there exists a divine will to create a striving, a drive, towards ideals. That is all the truer when the idea of *perfecting* is privileged, as it often is in these moralities and religions, over the idea of *perfection*. Perfection is considered divine, and the ability to perfect oneself, human.

Nonetheless, people still don't say that, in this striving and drive towards stated ideals, there are ethnic groups who have roles to play, and who are privileged. Over this point, we must linger, as we are about to do, over the problems that the Covenant and Election have posed to all thinkers enamored of universality. If the mission is given to the whole world, then the whole world is Jewish, and Israel becomes the symbolic name for the global nation that is taking shape, and that is on the way to sanctity. At any rate, during the time it takes for this nation to perfect itself, it would become Jewish. One could say that the Judaization of every human being in the world belongs to a striving towards a just and merciful God. At once the specter of Saint Paul threatens Judaism and dissolves its singularity. How can one emerge from this shadow to be eternally unique, eternally universal? That is the subject of this book.

Recourse to the Scripture In the Bible, several verses in Deuteronomy emphasize the importance of the privilege granted Israel, source of the amazed gratitude of this people for the honor rendered it. God chose to *love* a small—"unimposing"—people, the smallest of peoples, and He chose to choose it. But Israel, chosen for reasons it does not know, must surely not boast about having been chosen. Despite itself, it has benefited

the Jewish Prison
Jean Daniel

from an almost fortuitous—or in any case arbitrary—love, a gift of grace, so it should be full of gratitude. It is from this gratitude that obedience to the divine laws should follow. God creates a specific, unique relationship with His Chosen People. The Creator, at first disappointed by His creation, suddenly creates a people and He weds what He has created. But, in order for God to love Himself in His people, He must above all not regret His love. The Covenant must not be degraded or betrayed by the behavior of its covenanters.

From that moment forward, everything takes place as if the condemnation of Israel to permanent adoration rendered all the sins of this people more serious than the sins of all other peoples. These sins in effect bear witness to a failure to comprehend, or at the very least to an underestimation of the Nuptials that God chose to celebrate with Israel, and constitute the unpardonable offense of His spouses. Israel is not free to be ungrateful. By loving Israel, God deprives it of its liberty.

It is true that the authors of Deuteronomy keep adding corrections, mutually contradictory at times, to the most attractive interpretations they had previously suggested. Since the laws of God are universal, since they concern all humanity, to the love of God is added a form of freedom that lets one accomplish, well or ill, the received mission of truth and prophecy. Later on in the prophetic literature born after the First Exile we find—in Isaiah especially—

the idea that, as a result (or because?) of the immense difficulty of answering God's intense love, by obeying His commandments, Israel could be, according to Leopold Senghor's phrase, a "people suffering" for all the nations. Already, in the Pentateuch, the authors of Leviticus emphasized that God, the source and protector of the Covenant, cannot withdraw His love, even after punishing those He had chosen. Finally, the rabbis cite Exodus to show that "the Election of Israel is based on its free and voluntary acceptance of the Torah on Mount Sinai." It is from this moment of acceptance that one could say that Israel chose a voluntary servitude and renounced its former freedom. According to this interpretation, it is Israel that has decided to build its prison, the conception of which has been offered to it, and in which it will imprison itself of its own free will. And it will do this for all time, for, as Leo Strauss said, "the permanence of Judaism bears witness to the fact that there will never be a Redemption."

The Choice of Servitude

Here an interpretation—bold in itself—plays an important part in my argument. Those who are called "the rabbis"— the Talmudic commentators on the unwritten Law that allows for an interpretation of the written Law—go so far as to imagine that the Torah might have been freely offered in the first place to all the nations of the world. Not to one people that had been chosen as first of all, but to all peoples. Each of these nations would then have refused, because of the "extreme severity" of its rules that threatened their way of life. Only Israel, according to them, volunteered. Thus Israel would have taken part in its own Election, would have chosen to be Chosen.

This is a bold assertion in that it evokes the possibility of a relief on the paths of asceticism and sanctity. Israel thus decides to live according to the Law and by so doing to fulfill the terrible mission the Law includes. God's choice would thus be the fruit of a just reward for the merit of one people, and the acknowledgement of the cowardliness of all the others who become, because of just this, inferior in His eyes. No longer is it an Election decided by God; now it is a free discipleship chosen by a people different from the others. This same people would have proven themselves worth of being loved by God and chosen by Him, before God distinguished—or even created—it from among all the nations.

Of course one may well, as I will do later, wonder if this people did not overestimate its strength by taking on commitments that it would be forced to betray at every moment. The fact remains that this hypothesis does not in any way (quite the contrary) diminish the imprisonment. Israel freely chose for itself a fate from which it and its descendants would no longer be able to escape. I will keep repeating it: One can only be recaptured by one's fate.

The original freedom would disappear in the sands of oblivion. When it becomes a memory forcing one to obsess on it, it is linked with the accumulated burdens of the past. This freedom becomes no more than a story of destiny, and a recollection of the privilege of servitude.

An Infinite and Merciless Love

This interpretation forcefully emphasizes the fact that only absolute obedience to the Law makes Israel a singular, unique, and irreplaceable people that can thus, correctly, be thought of as chosen—the English expression *chosen people* better conveys faithfulness to divine intentions, say scholars, than the French "*peuple élu.*" Whether the people were chosen or proved themselves worthy of being so, the fact remains that the Covenant was made with this people, and sanctified by the ritual ceremonies of sacrifice, including the circumcision of Abraham at the age of ninety, of Ishmael at the age of twelve, and of Isaac, ten days old.

Although himself cut off from the synagogue, Spinoza emphasized the almost absolute nature of the transmission of that irreversible sign, imprinted in the flesh, and symbolizing the promise: "I attribute so much value to the sign of circumcision, that by itself alone I judge it capable of ensuring this nation an eternal existence."

Even if God rewarded a unique, exceptional merit, we are guilty of not proving ourselves worthy of it. We live beneath the yoke accepted by our ancestors, and the tradition of this aristocracy of the Chosen becomes hereditary, transmitted to all generations for centuries and centuries to come. Is it possible to escape because one believes oneself unworthy? Is it possible, in short, to stop being Jewish according to the initial definitions of the word? In no way.

Yet in fact, the majority of Jews are not Jewish by the standards of the commission they received. They are left with declarations of belonging, observations of rites, a feeling of arrogance when facing the fact that they are chosen and a feeling of guilt or revolt when faced with the fact that they do not deserve it. So that a certain victim condition has imposed itself on the Jews, to punish their unworthiness regularly. Only the converted and the nonbelievers could free themselves from the servitudes of testimony and priesthood: "I will make You into a holy nation, a kingdom of priests."

But if God, emerging from eternity, creating Time which He enters and Space which He fills with His creations, decides to create a people starting from one man, Abraham, who was expecting none of this, who had neither ambition nor illumination—a man who sees himself forced to leave "his land, his country, his family, his house"—then it's God Himself who imprisons His chosen within His blessing, with all the infinite power and majesty of an eternal love.

Furthermore, God wants to be loved—and Claudel will feign surprise that so many Christians have saved their love for Christ, about whom it has been said that he was more loved than loving. God stresses what Israel owes Him and how He, God, has been faithful to the Covenant, just as the flight from Egypt seals the Covenant, which constitutes the commemoration of it. He gives and gives again, speaks and speaks again, recalls and repeats the reasons to be faithful to Him. He ends up, sovereign and threatening, telling Israel: "If you do not love me, beware!"

The Obligation of Holiness Modern exegetes, eager to rejuvenate the meaning of Election, or adapt it to our moral code, have tried to separate the notion of *difference* from that of *superiority*. To avoid the arrogance that the fact of being chosen can arouse, they demonstrate that one can draw pride only from a *deserved Election*. Superiority could only consist in praising God and observing the Law. And, says Levinas, even this notion of superiority is found to be deprived of meaning insofar as the prophet suffers from the solitude of his prophecy. God tells Moses to tell the Pharaoh that Israel is His *first-born*, but not His *only child*.

This indicates a chronological precedence in the accession of nations to existence. A choice could not have been offered to nations that did not exist. But we understand that it is not a question of judging a theological coherence. Only the tormented life that the problems of Divine Election inspire in the Chosen concerns us.

the Jewish Prison
Jean Daniel

To return to the notion of superiority, as separate from that of *difference*, let us recall that Maimonides assigns poverty a sort of preeminence. If one is not born to poverty, one can still choose to *deserve* it in proving one's faithfulness to the Covenant. This is a path to sanctity. In the Bible whatever and whoever is *devoted to God* is holy and close to God. In the Temple, the priests were supposed to have a privileged relationship with God, and, by maintaining spiritual purity, deserved the term "holy." In fact, this term was reserved for Moses, David, Samuel, Elijah, Elisha: "They all acted under the influence and authority of God."

What does that signify? It is not a matter, here, of the Promised Land. If you want to respect the Covenant, if you want to be a Jew conforming to the Covenant, you must be a witness or a priest. "Witness" means a just man. "Priest" signifies prophesying or preaching. Apart from those two aspects, there is no Judaism.

I yearn for someone to lecture me on the universality of Judaism, but only if he respects the significance of the Covenant, which is quite strict. Not everyone can be Jewish; it is an extremely difficult task. Once again, Judaism is a summons to holiness. The same questions keep coming back to this crucial point. Didn't God invest these men with an inhuman mission? If men take the fact, the privilege, of having been singled out, and use it to behave in a way that arouses hatred and persecution even indirectly, what becomes of the "mission"? Can't this condemnation to Election be thought of as the flip side of a "malediction"?

Election, in any event, brings more theoretical aporias with it than empirical deliverance.

The Land and the Sacred   In the Bible, however, the notions of Election and holiness experience a similar evolution, steadily taking on an ever more moral, "spiritualized" sense. Contrary to the so-called "historical" books, the Prophets will reverse the possible divine "disfavor," the "reprobation of Heaven," in an appeal for a renewing of the Covenant, whose gratuitous and irrevocable nature they emphasize. The prophets themselves never think of themselves as "chosen." It is God who reveals Himself to be unfailing. The idea of a "holy nation" is erased before that of the "holy seed" or "remnant" of Israel. The heart, and not the Temple, becomes the place of God, or at least of His presence and His revelation. The separation that holiness implies is from then on, and above all, asserted as a rupture with the sacral, that is to say with the deification of any part of the Creation or of History that might be compared to the idolatry of the pagans.

The destruction of the second Temple, at the beginning of the Christian era, tragically confirms this double movement. Of all the schools of thought that existed at the time—the Sadducees, the Essenes, the Hellenizing Jews of Alexandria, etc.—only rabbinical and synagogal Pharisaism would survive, at once the most affirming of identity and also the most appropriate to the conditions of the diaspora. Contrary to Christianity, another spiritualized form of worship but one based on the concrete universality of an openness to all nations, this Judaism would keep the singular meaning of Election by asserting both the abstract universality of the Law and the privilege of the limited fraternity that it alone had received. The aporia, renewed, would only find an eschatological resolution: At the end of times, peoples will turn towards Jerusalem, "Zion of the Holy One of Israel," as Isaiah says.

This rejection of all idolatry, including the rejection of any sacred status of the Land, explains the initial hostility between Zionists and the religious—which certain Hassidic groups continue to show today in Israel. This rejection also nourishes praise for the status of the diaspora as the exile described by thinkers such as George Steiner, or the scholar Esther Benbassa.

The Spinoza Rebellion

In a certain sense, Spinoza was the first to rebel against the claim of the Jewish people in believing it alone was chosen, and thus also against the claim of scholars of the Law in believing that they alone were invested with the mission of showing why the Jewish people was chosen.

In his entry in the *Encyclopedia Universalis*, Emmanuel Levinas is obviously thinking of Spinoza, without citing him, when he refutes the traditional notion of Election. Levinas says—magnificently—that everyone can join and become part of the chosen people; that this Election does not create an aristocracy of the privileged; that one is chosen for the arduous tasks of superior, supernumerary duties, not for the proud enjoyment of benefiting from a divine caprice. Does this apply in wartime too?

The Jews, according to Levinas, are only priests condemned to the thankless and terrible calling of showing God's intention to humanity. These priests are "different" from others only in the number of tasks and sufferings that are their lot. Others point out that the people is chosen only to occupy the function of priests and witnesses, and not to lead a State, or an army. Priest and witness, and nothing else, to be an example and nothing more. One is not chosen to enjoy something superior to others; one is chosen to be an example for others, to bear witness to a human universal.

Once again: Is this compatible with war?

We know that Spinoza, influenced, as they say, by Juan De Prado, had formerly professed "libertine and atheistic" opinions, which earned him enmity and excommunication from the Jewish community of Amsterdam and from his own family. We are less aware that, in 1660, Spinoza was wounded by a knife thrown by a fanatical Jew who was exhibiting his membership in the chosen people in a rather special way. There comes a time, in fact, when our questioning of the meaning of a religious message must deal with both the way it is inspired, and also with the way it is received, understood, and applied by the faithful.

If Election is indeed what Levinas says it is, then not only is there no more problem of being chosen, but we can also be led to believe that there is no more Election. For the Jewish people would be chosen by God in order to produce heroes and saints. Certainly that permits us to understand His divine wish to keep pure and authentic the particular qualities reserved for the elect of His choosing. But, as we have seen quite often in the course of this essay, that would also pose the whole human, too-human, question of whether it is possible to be a hero as well as a saint.

The Model and its Rivals

It is not just the Jewish fate, then, that led me to reflect upon Election. It is observing the adventures and noting the misfortunes that, throughout history, have almost always followed the fact of an individual, a group, or a faith when they believe themselves unique in being able to interpret God, History, Tradition, the Race, the Revolution. Always the same expressions and references. These men were visited, or inspired, or marked; they believe in their dream, in their star, in their fortune, or in their luck;

they have a unique system to explain the world and they develop it (either under dictation from the gods, or under the inspiration of their genius) in books that their disciples make sacred; and then, as an ultimate consequence, more serious than all the others, they feel the need to struggle, with all available weapons, against their enemies, who can only be those who resist them.

That, you will agree, is something of an abbreviated version of Election, a concept that is far from belonging to the Jewish people alone, even if it has been incarnated by them more than by others. Thus, if we are indeed dealing with an anthropological constant, the historical forms of it remain unequal. Filiation, substitution, negation, borrowing with or without competition: Depending on whether one goes from the theological domain to the political domain or from traditional societies to modern times, the scene keeps changing. Only the wish to be chosen remains invariable.

The Christian Reversal   As to the other two monotheisms, Christian and Muslim, the notion of Election plays a large role in them, but one that conflicts with the Jewish definition. The New Testament applies the term "chosen" by turns to Jesus, to the Church, and to the believer. In the Gospel of John, especially, the incarnation of the eternal *Logos* is equivalent to the entry into Messianic times: The Son of God and

the Jewish Prison
Jean Daniel

the Son of Man turns out to be the descendant of David who had been expected, at once the royal anointed one and suffering servant. His message—which above all concerns Himself and the news of His coming into the world—is thus addressed to all the nations. They are summoned to form the *ecclesia*, to which the first epistle attributed to Peter applies the descriptions of Israel usual in the Bible: "kingdom of priests, holy nation, chosen people." The difference in fact lies with the believer, whose faith is required as an absolute condition and which remains dependent on the obligation of an entirely personal judgment: Election, as Peter says again, but in the Second Epistle, is a "calling" subject to verification.

Paul-Saul, a Pharisee who was first a persecutor and then was converted on the road to Damascus, invents nothing, then. On the contrary, his epistle to the Romans, at the heart of the New Testament, shows the Christian renewal of the paradox and aporia of the Election confronting the mystery of Israel, and even more the paradox of maintaining and persevering in Judaism despite the arrival (in his opinion) of the Messiah. For Paul, the Jews' being chosen is irreversible, while, at the same time, their rejection remains an enigma to him—hence the somewhat muddled quality of this epistle, interpretations of which, through the ages, become increasingly distorted and hostile.

It is with the Fathers of the Church, and especially after the peace of Constantine in the fourth century, that we encounter a theological anti-Judaism that, despite the highly polemical dimension of the question, is difficult to compare with modern anti-Semitism. A phrase by Augustine sums it up better than anything else: "The Jews carry Books that they do not understand." The "No" of the Synagogue to the Church follows a fracture line that will bring to bear theological-political measures. In the name of a henceforth dominant Christianity, which makes itself out to be "the True Israel" (the substitution theory), the Emperor Justinian includes the Jews in his global repression of minorities. With the discovery that the Book of the Jews is not so much the Bible as the Talmud, and that the Talmud also has its share of anti-Christianity, the Latin Middle Ages from the thirteenth century forward will legalize and generalize the use of persecution and discrimination.

The position of the Catholic Church scarcely changed on this point until the Second Vatican Council, when this "teaching of contempt" was officially abandoned. But it wasn't until Pope John Paul II, the former bishop of Krakow, that significant gestures were made: a visit to the synagogue in Rome, recognition by the Vatican of the State of Israel, pilgrimage to the Wailing Wall, and Repentance for centuries of hostility. The characterization of the Jews as "elder brothers" annulled the theory of "the True Israel" by recognizing, as Paul did, the irreversibility of the first Election, without, however, renouncing the validity of the second. If the political progress of this is unquestionable,

the Jewish Prison
Jean Daniel

the theological aporia on this question still remains the double motive, as in the Epistle to the Romans, that animates the most recent book by Jean-Marie Lustiger, entitled precisely *La Promesse*, in which the cardinal warns that he will displease both the Jews and the Catholics.

Concerning the State of Israel, we should keep in mind the important "pastoral directives" that the French Episcopal Committee promulgated on April 16, 1973. This is a signal text that testifies to the difficulty of "passing a serene judgment on the return of the Jewish people to its land." Michel Renaud quotes the preamble to these pastoral directives: "First of all we cannot forget, as Christians, the gift made long ago by God to the people of Israel of a land upon which it has been summoned to reunite" (*cf.* Gen 12:7; 26:3-4; 28:13; Is 43:5-7; Jer 16:15; Zeph 3:20). The first mention of the gift of land immediately gives way to the calling of Abraham: "[T]hey went forth to go into the land of Canaan; and into the land of Canaan they came. And Abram passed through the land unto the place of Sichem, unto the plain of Moreh. And the Canaanite *was* then in the land. And the Lord appeared unto Abram, and said, Unto thy seed will I give this land" (Gen. 12:5-8). We should remember this. After Babylon, people would often refuse to do so. Even before it existed, Abraham's posterity was linked, by the word of God, to the land of Canaan. From the beginning of the history of the patriarchs, the people and the land will be joined by one single divine promise, and this promise, presented as irrevocable, is confirmed to Isaac and to Jacob. The *Pastoral Orientations* of the French bishops confirmed this at a time when John-Paul II solemnly recognized the State of Israel.

The Ambivalence of the Koran

In the Koran, the matter is presented quite differently. The choosing of a Prophet or believer is a pure act of the absolute will of God. In the omniscience that is His, He predestines the one He has chosen to the state of submission by distinguishing him from the infidel. The radical theological requirement is such that by Islamic law, membership in the *Umma*, the community of believers, is irrevocable, and any apostate member accordingly is punished with death. But it also has a theological consequence for the very heart of Biblical history. Whereas Christianity claims to fulfill the Jewish Election by encompassing all nations within it, Islam postulates, against both Judaism and Christianity, that, though it is the latest arrival, it is no less ancient than they because of its ontological coincidence with the original Abrahamic foundation. From then on, the Jews have not only been surpassed as "chosen people," but also, in a way, become usurpers who yet must be protected.

the Jewish Prison
Jean Daniel

The ambivalence of Election is more fraught, then: The Koran can both call the Jews to witness the truth of the *final* revelation made to Mohammed, or also treat them as "falsifiers of the Scriptures." This ambivalence is resolved through the theological-political status of *dhimmi*, or non-denominational citizenship, considered inferior but tolerated, and even guaranteed, and granted equally to the other "peoples of the Book," that is, the Jews, the Zoroastrians, and the Christians. Since the welcome given to the Sephardic Jews after their expulsion from Spain in 1492—an expulsion into the heart of an Ottoman Empire founded on the equilibrium of minorities—was real, then clearly the status of *dhimmi* needed no improvement.

In modern times, because of their absence of demands for a nation, the Jews suffered less than the Christians. But, after the second half of the nineteenth century, with the appearance first of solidarity movements among European Jews, and then of Zionism, the Arab-Muslim world witnessed the rebirth of a virulent anti-Semitism often modeled, because of colonization, on that of the West. The founding of the State of Israel precipitated this movement.

Borrowings Beyond the conflicts of filiation between the three monotheisms, the notion of Election has gone through many changes, and has been invoked under either a collective or an individual form. The idea of a holy kingdom derived from

Biblical Israel gave rise to several different interpretations. Among Eastern forms of Christianity, Armenian identity shares most similarity with Judaism. Armenian ethnicity, land, language, culture, exile, diaspora, faith, and awareness of genocide are all comparable to Judaism's. Similarly, as the Armenian kingdom was the first to convert to Christianity in the third century, before being swept up many times by the shock of empires throughout history, the Republic of Armenia was among the first to declare its independence during the collapse of the USSR. Ethiopia, which wants to be both African and Semitic, for its part, reinvented itself as the youngest child of the chosen people. Ethiopia claims to be the outcome of the love affair of Solomon with the Queen of Sheba, and the final resting-place for the Ark of the Covenant which their son Menelik, descendant of David, is said to have transferred to Axum, the ancient capital. Centuries later, in the heart of the Middle Ages, a priest-king founded a holy city on the high plateaus and gave his name to it. This was Lalibela, the new Zion, where the river was called Jordan, where people go to pray over the presumed tomb of Abraham, and where the highest nearby mountain is called Sinai. But, closer to us, these borrowings also conditioned the sacred history of the West: If France can declare itself "eldest daughter of the Church," it's because the Capetian kings portrayed, on cathedral stained-glass windows, the tree of Jesse, in which they too found their place, their branch of the Davidic dynasty. In fact, each time what we witness is the desire of a nation to graft itself onto sacred history: By filiation and substitution, one is assured of Election. This mimetic process may or may not be competitive.

This wish for a providential design is magnified in its imperial form, where Messianic hope foretells a world unified under perpetual peace and thus approaching the eschatological vision of all the peoples of the earth turning around a sacred center. By donning the royal purple, Charlemagne, himself an offspring of the barbarian invasions, disputes with Byzantium the inheritance of pagan, then Christian, Romanity, in order to win the title "lieutenant of God." By striving to extend the Germanic Holy Roman Empire, Frederick I (Barbarossa) was laying down the foundations of Europe's future while continually questioning the Pope's magistracy. A little earlier, at the beginning of the first millennium, by adopting Orthodoxy, medieval Russia thought it could save Christianity, which it saw was debased by the Latin Church; soon, after the fall of Constantinople, it claimed to be "the Third Rome." In the midst of the Age of Enlightenment, Frederick II of Prussia justified his annexations by referring to the notion of Election as God defined it. And, quite close to us, the United States of America combines democratic liberalism with biblical inspiration in a civil religion—*one nation under God*—whose ethical universalism is supposed to guarantee their status as a superpower, since God reserved the New World expressly for this Reign of Good.

The collective dimension of Election does not often stray from some individual embodiment of it. When de Gaulle says, "What Alexander calls his fate, Caesar his luck, and Napoleon his star," he is referring to the idea that the man of destiny, by establishing himself as master of History, thinks of himself as a chosen man. When Napoleon enters Jena, Hegel thinks he sees "Reason on horseback" passing by. But borrowing from the myth of Election turns into nightmare when the imperial adventure substitutes for the body of revelation some laicized religion of a totalitarian form. By divinizing race or class in various ways, Nazism and Stalinism activated a terror machine without precedent solely for the glory of bloodthirsty tyrants promoted to the rank of idols. History then takes the place of God, and chooses its principal agent on Earth by communicating its attributes to him. And the different interpreters of Revolution, whether they be National Socialist, Marxist, or Islamic, claim this demiurgic privilege by claiming that their mission is to create a new humanity.

All terrorist groups subscribe to these philosophies, implicitly or explicitly. To tell the truth, it is by thinking about them, and about violence, that I encountered this concept and its tragic richness. The lesson is already there in Dostoyevsky. In *Crime and Punishment*, Raskolnikov believes he can match the Election of the great man, in this case Napoleon, by killing an old woman for no reason. In *The Devils*, Kirilov thinks both that he becomes God and that he demonstrates atheism by killing himself after committing atrocious crimes. Do the people who send the young *mujahadeen* to their death by transforming them into human bombs think any differently?

The temptation to shatter the world in an apocalyptic explosion is strong. Martin Buber has even written a surprising novel about this, *For the Sake of Heaven*, which tells how the masters of Hasidism in the depths of Eastern Europe, having heard of Napoleon (him again), try to combine their mystical powers so that the ordeal of fire forces the Messiah to manifest, "hastening the end." None of them would survive this wish to force God's hand.

*Against
Judeocentrism*

I encountered the problem of Election whenever I came up against the wishes of unbelieving Jews to assert their Jewish uniqueness. In my naivety, I thought it obvious that the Jewish religion could only be, for certain people, an identity based on faith and that, once distanced from it, each person was free to live a national identity alien to any reckonings that are Biblical in their historicity, or to assurances of a Promised Land.

After the genocide, and after the foundation of Israel, this distinction between believers and non-believers became inoperative. We began to think that anti-Semitism could take a thousand different forms. But in this perspective, in the eyes of the anti-Semites, the Jews were always, tirelessly, the same. Judaism was presented not as a choice but as a form of *belonging*, not as an adherence but as a *fate*. There was, forged in the unparalleled catastrophes of genocide, an identity that did not necessarily depend on God but that led to a *condition*. To want to leave this Jewish condition was unrealistic and suspicious—all the more so when the greatest minds that bore the honor of Jewish genius were proud of such belonging, whatever might be the cost. How could this luminous pride be associated with the tragic quality of that condition? It was simple. The answer is obvious. By Election.

Election amounted to making the Jewish question a central pole of thought. Judeocentrism is overtly expressed by the fact that, for instance, in the ghettos of Poland, where, whenever something happened—whether it was an overlord falling from his horse or one of his conjugal misfortunes—Jews wondered: "Is it good for us or not?" There it was a question of a *Judeocentrism of protection*. And it's a fact that persecution reinforces the legitimacy of such a recourse. But there is moreover a *Judeocentrism of reflection* that leads, often implicitly, sometimes explicitly, to considering the Jew as the witness, the experimentalist, the prophet of all nations, and that comes to him from the Covenant. The assertion of the singularity of the Jewish people, the wish to remain unique, the fear of being dissolved in a society of others, the absence of proselytism, although corrected by the imposing number of mixed marriages, the conviction that one can only be exemplary if one is particular, all these ideas make it possible for us to speak of a philosophy of Judeocentrism. But instinctively, impulsively, or because of my upbringing, I have always wanted to escape from this notion.

Eternity of
Anti-Semitism?

If Israel is a fate, how can it be escaped? If Oedipus is tragic, it's because he could not refuse his fate. Are we condemned to tragedy? What does it remind us of, this singular story of an Election that arouses all misfortunes and then our protests against these misfortunes? If certain Jews, Judas in particular, allowed Christ to reveal himself to men, made possible the process that goes from kerygma to Passion and Resurrection, why, in the name of this logic, should we deny that the executioners of the Jewish people contribute to its mission? What mockery! What an impasse! What sound and fury inspired within the oldest of vicious circles in the revealed religions. What should we be faithful to? Must we follow the famous commandment and leave our country, our community, our family, in order the better to return to non-earthly roots? The answer is perhaps in the simplicity of our everyday behavior.

Should everything be rethought, starting with the realization of the Zionist ideal? Can the interpretation of anti-Semitism remain the same for one who has done battle as it is for one persecuted just for being what he is? Doesn't the difference between "doing" and "being" have effect here? This is not just an essential question, it is *the* question. It is proper for us to keep returning to it. For we must emphasize once again that, since the appearance of a sovereign Hebrew State, the Jews, and more precisely the Israelis, are entirely responsible for their acts. They no longer depend only on their will and their ideal. They are henceforth acting protagonists, and they recognize themselves as such. This observation should spoil the argument of the supporters of a theory of an eternal anti-Semitism. But there are many Jews, Zionist or not, who refuse to make a list of the precise causes of anti-Semitism. They mean to point out the long historical continuity of it, and they privilege a "trans-historical reading of anti-Semitism." They ascribe the "permanence of hatred to an anti-Semitic essence peculiar to every non-Jew," as Denis Charbit summarizes it in his *Anthologie des sionismes* (Anthology of Zionisms). And Leon Pinsker, no doubt out of "professional bias" (he was a doctor by training), in his essay that was influential on Zionist thinking, "Auto-Emancipation: An Appeal to His People by a Russian Jew," published anonymously in Berlin in 1882, defined hatred of Jews, "Judeophobia," as a "psychic aberration. As a psychic aberration it is hereditary, and as a disease transmitted for two thousand years it is incurable."[2]

These defenders give me the impression of belonging to a pre-Darwinian era. Before Darwin gave an origin to the species, before he attributed evolution to them, time really did not exist in the sciences. Before Darwin, the sciences had a fixed subject. Darwin introduced time into science. The theoreticians of eternal anti-Semitism do not introduce time into either the observer or the observed. Neither the Jew nor the anti-Semite changes. Only the masks that conceal the anti-Semites metamorphose.

Reopening
History

The question has often been posed: Is it the Jews who provoke the reaction of rejection, or do they shape themselves in response to the hostility that hounds them? When the Jews are persecuted, they have a tendency to essentialize the hostility, that is to say they make anti-Semitism into a category of the mind—of the mind of others, as if it were different from their own. When they are in periods of happiness, they have the tendency either to reduce their singularity or to take advantage of it as of a kind of superiority. This attitude is obviously contrary to the command as defined by the most exigent commentators, such as Yeshayahu

---

[2] See the text online at *www.jewishvirtuallibrary.org/jsource/Zionism/pinsker.html*

Leibowitz, Emmanuel Levinas, or Martin Buber, in the following terms: "You are not chosen; you must deserve to be chosen." The Jews are, as it were, assigned to isolation, and, in any case, to difference.

In *Dieu est-il fanatique?* (Is God a Fanatic?) I developed the idea that it was unhealthy for the mind, for the balance of one's reason, to think that there is a mysterious dimension to anti-Semitism. We have to live as if it didn't exist, while still telling ourselves it might possibly be there. This attitude that I have decided to make my own is very difficult to justify. There are people who say that there is a metaphysics of anti-Semitism and that to deny it would be to deny its ontology. But, in the very name of the Bible, we are right to challenge these essentialist views, which are actually Greek at bottom, and to prefer instead the vision of an open history.

III.
the Shoah

I have said to corruption, Thou *art* my
father: to the worm, *Thou art* my mother,
and my sister.
And where *is* now my hope?

Job 17:14-15.

Election according to merit or superiority, Covenant that includes promises and a protection: The fact remains that the people that will go on to call itself Israel will be confronted with Evil and with the problems posed by Evil in all the monotheisms to come. It is often emphasized that the destructions of the Temple (586 B.C.E. and 70 C.E.) and the failure of the Jewish revolt against the Romans led by Shimon bar-Kokhba (132-135 C.E.) led the Jews to rethink the role of God in the Covenant. Was God absent? Could He have been? The "rabbis" introduced important questions that would resurface during the Christian persecutions and even more so after Auschwitz.

Does God punish? Does He punish those He blames for no longer loving Him and for forgetting His Law? Why doesn't He guide His people away from the possibility of disobeying? Of committing evil? Of risking the punishments that He, God, decides to inflict? Of undergoing finally the tragedy of such punishments? And, a modern question: Why afterwards should we punish those who were only the instruments of divine justice or of Election? Finally, a question posed in this essay: If God punishes those who do not manage to be priests or witnesses or saints, is the flip side of the Election of the few the curse of everyone?

In the Talmud we find that "suffering must be understood as forming part of the process of redemption." Although Levinas excludes any theological justification for the catastrophe experienced by his people, speaking of "useless suffering" that nothing can appease, he several times uses the term "Passion" to designate what the Jews (he also says Judaism) experienced between 1940 and 1945: "The Passion when everything was consumed, and this boldness of beginning again [that the Zionist undertaking of founding a State represents]..., were experienced as signs of the same Election or of the same curse, that is to say of the same exceptional fate." This statement too is often cited: "The memory of the Passion experienced by Judaism between 1940 and 1945 restored awareness of their exceptional fate to men who, just thirty years ago, seemed to house the totality of their existence in the clearly defined Western categories of nation, State, art, social class, and profession (and sometimes even religion, though rarely)." Annette Wieviorka, in *Déportation et Génocide*, observes that "there is often in the narratives an identification of the Jews with Christ. 'Jew, it's your turn to carry the Cross,' exclaims a deportee, Suzanne Birnbaum."

Concerning this attitude, Emmanuel Levinas, in *Influence de Spinoza*, which is at my side throughout this book, makes this brilliant and disdainful commentary: "Useful cliché! The master of the Gospels attracts [the Jews], medieval history rejects [them]. How many efforts have been made since then to look in the Palestinian landscapes for the trace of his footsteps, the salt of his tears, the echo of the prayers of the one they call the last *prophet of Israel* .... To how many Jewish intellectuals, detached from any religious belief, does the figure of Jesus seem the accomplishment of the teachings of the prophets?"

That was true before the Shoah. Since then, Jesus does not bring any sort of adequate explanation.

From the Book to Books It is the transcendental interpretation of the Shoah in its ahistorical dimension and in its relationship with the creation of the Jewish State that removes the Israeli-Palestinian conflict from the confines of the study of war and from commentaries on the conquest aspect of the return to Zion. Deuteronomy also asserts, in the same spirit, that the Covenant is eternal, but that the life or death of the Chosen People depends on their observance of the Law. From then on, when the Babylonian exile occurs, the question is posed, and the Bible will ask, whether the "God of hosts" was conquered, whether the "jealous God" is

the Jewish Prison
Jean Daniel

unjust, whether "the God of promise" is unfaithful. The answer of the prophets is that God shines forth in His sovereignty by the proof of the confidence to which He subjects His people, which invites them to a renewal of their Espousals. But, there again, the discourse divides in two: Prophecies of the return to Zion contrast with prophecies of divine retribution—an opposition that is often found in the same prophet (Ezekiel) with his famous dream of the bones that, reunited, proclaim the Resurrection.

The message is then taken up again in an apocalyptic mode, as in those visions of the same Ezekiel where the threats of total destruction are tempered only by the perspective of a Messianic rebirth, even of an eschatological resurrection. But, in all these cases, calamity is integrated into the sacred story, the severity of divine pedagogy being increasingly likened to the proof of a radical love.

As to genocide, it is such an enormous punishment that it rarely inspired such commentaries. Significantly, when the time of witness comes, and when the literature of the camps comes into play, especially from the 1960's onwards, the authors are for the most part Jewish "laypeople." That in itself conveys a sociological fact. But not just that. The rabbis that Elie Wiesel describes to us in the Nazi camps were themselves completely overwhelmed. Just as much as the others. These devotees of Hassidism suddenly discover themselves deprived of their usual religious reference points. The silence to which they are reduced accompanies the silence of God.

If theoretic publications on this subject soon become abundant, the testimonies and narratives of a religious kind remain rare, and appear late. A fine example of this is Sylvain Kaufmann's *Le Livre de la mémoire* (The book of memory), published in the early 1990's. This Jew from Alsace, born under German rule, grew up as strictly observant, and with a love of France; he escaped from Auschwitz and took care to describe his experience in the present tense in order to demonstrate that, all throughout his ordeal, and despite the absolute horror of it, he had remained under the gaze of God and with full confidence in His providence. Accordingly, the explanation he gives takes up the Biblical schema in full: Divine punishment for infidelity turns into a miracle with the return of the Promised Land and the founding of the State of Israel; because of this, Election endures, however tragic its detours. As unusual as this point of view seems in the literature, it is not certain that we should consider it isolated. It is, in a certain way, the opposite position to that of Primo Levi who, revealing the void, lets only vertigo survive.

The Madness of Rather than in personal testimonies and narratives, religious
Understanding interpretation came to manifest itself in commentaries—

again, appearing late on the scene—often addressing the theory of the "silence of God," which sometimes open fractures in the heart of the Jewish world that have causes other than the Shoah. We should mention, if only because of the scandal they caused, the recent declarations of the important Rabbi Ovadiah Josef, spiritual guide of the Sephardic party Shas, which were later taken up by a major French rabbi. According to Josef, the victims of the Shoah were none other than the reincarnated souls of those men and women who, at Sinai, had worshipped the Golden Calf and were thus justly punished. Leaving aside the doctrine of reincarnation, which exists in the Kabbalistic tradition, as well as the resentment within Israel against the Ashkenazim that this suggestion implies, this kind of vision of a God who is not only vengeful but also capable of infinite cruelty is an instance of the horror of terrorism, in the true meaning of the word.

It is in quite a different way that Rav Adin Steinsaltz—a solitary figure in Israel, regarded as the "new Rashi" because of his monumental translation of the Talmud into various modern languages (including Hebrew, English, French, and Russian), but one who is also an intellectual adept at contemporary debate and capable of conversation with Sartre or Levinas—distinguishes himself from interpretations that are at once fundamentalist and secular. In his opinion, the imprecations of the prophets refer less to an active divine will than to the reality of History, which becomes even more tragic when we stop considering it as a sacred history. Without making himself the interpreter of divine providence, he emphasizes the unique dimension of the Jewish fate marked by unfathomable tragedies. Then, and without minimizing the event of the Shoah, he nonetheless refuses the capacity of that event to impose silence on God. The question of Evil, especially, seems to him (and in this respect he is similar to Dostoyevsky in *The Brothers Karamazov*) fully posed by the death—even natural—of a single child. Even more than the catastrophes, including the inconceivable ones, that can affect the Jewish peoples from without, Rav Steinsaltz urges instead that we fear a process of disappearance that can lead to the abandonment, the non-transmission, the loss, of Talmudic tradition, a tradition that, for him, has comprised and continues to comprise, all by itself, the continuity of the Jewish condition.

A Negative Sacrality? But most of the other religious commentators (Jewish or Christian) who are ready to see fits of Yahweh's rage in the destructions of the Temple, the Inquisition, and the pogroms—even if that means rediscovering His love through the misfortunes inflicted on their persecutors—still recoil at the idea of ascribing the Shoah to the righteous wrath of their God. The writings on the world of the concentration camps become part of the heritage of the sufferings of humanity. Man reduced to the level of animal, so that he can better be killed as an animal. Utterly unique, without precedent, unthinkable in human terms, necessarily escaping any explanation that would be equivalent to an understanding, a sacralized phenomenon in stark relief, symbol of absolute Evil, it resembles nothing else we have known since the origins of life and Man. That is what has been thought, said, and written, in all forms and in all tones of voice. How can we escape from that? This is where all the importance of *uniqueness* is revealed. The phenomenon must be unique.

It is as if the horror, in order to be not just acknowledged, or even accepted, but merely inscribed in the possibilities of History, needed to be unique. We have gone from the search for meaning to the establishment of uniqueness, then from the postulate of uniqueness to the assertion of the exclusivity of these victims. The challenge that Nazi barbarity represents for rational and historical intelligence encourages the dogma of the sacred character of Auschwitz. The temptation is great to consider the genocide as a phenomenon that transcends History. And to mark that, it will be given a singular, specific name. The great Parisian liberal rabbi, Daniel Farhi, is quick to remind us that the word "Shoah" comes from the Bible, and that it is cited thirteen times there, including three times in the Book of Job alone.

Each time this word designates a cataclysm, a catastrophe, either personal or national, but, in the Book of Job, it is a question of a misfortune attributed to divine will. In France, the popularization—outside the Jewish community—of this term is thanks to Claude Lanzmann because of the repercussions of his immense film *Shoah*, as well as to Serge Klarsfeld and to his four volumes entitled *La Shoah en France*. In fact, the expression "Shoah" was probably adopted publicly, and officially, for the first time, in Jerusalem in 1953, during the creation of a central memorial created to perpetuate the memory of the six million Jews killed by the Nazis and their accomplices, as well as the memory of the acts of heroism committed notably by the fighters in the ghettos but also by the "Just of the Nations"—the memorial named Yad Vashem.

This event is so incomprehensible, so disproportionate to any human infraction, that we want to believe it came from nowhere. We called it "inhuman." But *inhuman* can mean *sub-human* or *superhuman*, hence *extra-human*. In that case, who is its author? That can only be God or the Devil. The Devil? Who, among the commentators on the Shoah, believes in the existence of the Devil? Then does only God remain? The idea that the genocide can come from God, as I have emphasized, is a horror. Some, in order not to believe God responsible, have resigned themselves to His impotence or to His indifference; He deserted us, they say.

the Jewish Prison
Jean Daniel

The Steiner
Parade

Along with what Hans Jonas and Vladimir Jankélévitch said, we know the words of Adorno on the impossibility of writing poetry after Auschwitz. But the attitude of George Steiner seems even more radical. He turns the question backward: How could it happen, as it did, that the same SS officer could listen to Mozart in the afternoon and torture people by nightfall? All culture, particularly European culture, and precisely as it exists in relationship to transcendence, is at stake. Trilingual from childhood, a master of reading, a commentator on the Western canon, a witness to the vanished Judaism of the *Bildung*, Steiner himself declares he came into the world in "inhuman times." Nothing, for him, can fill the abyssal void of the Shoah, which shows divine vacuity first of all. When he denounces the uniquely German genealogy of Nazism, for instance the Germanness of a Heidegger, it's Christianity that Steiner has in mind. Rather than the question of knowing why the Jews refused to see in Jesus of Nazareth their awaited Messiah, and without ignoring the ensemble of historic-critical answers, he prefers to propose the question of deliberate choice: The Jews preferred the curiosity, the turbulence, the nomadism that constituted the secret of their existence instead of the certainty, the boredom, the fixation that the realization of messianism represented. Suddenly, this "no" of theirs becomes the source of Christian hatred for the Jew. Double hatred. Hatred of self, since they converted, and hatred of the Jewish witnesses of their conversion. Outside of this theological genesis, according to him, the Shoah remains unthinkable. Paul, and then Augustine, Luther, Karl Barth, and Jacques Maritain would thus make the Jews the ransom for a humanity that, because of their refusal, they hold hostage. The Jew, for his part, exercises an "intolerable psychological pressure on Western consciousness" in three ways: by his monotheism that is as abstract as it is implacable, in which the Holy of Holies is discovered to be terrifyingly empty; by the Judaism that is latent and recurrent in the heart of Christianity; by the Marxist (egalitarian) messianism that must, according to Steiner, be thought of as an "impatient Judaism." The conjunction between this hatred, this pressure, and the shadowy elements of many centuries of oppression makes him establish a "symmetry between the eclipse of Golgotha and that black hole in history, the Shoah." The only outcome is the common escape, of both the Jew and the Christian, from the messianic horizon, their reciprocal "messianic abdication." For, if the Messiah came, says Steiner, we would have to tell him: "It is too late for you."

An Endless Solitude The position of Emil Fackenheim, the author of the most openly theological Jewish work grounded on the uniqueness

the Jewish Prison
Jean Daniel

of the Shoah, is illuminating on more than one account.
Taking support from Spinoza and Rosenzweig, but in order
to go beyond them, having recourse to Heidegger, but by
detaching him from his pre-war context, Fackenheim holds
that the centrality of the Holocaust makes God not so much
"dead" as "removed" from the history in which, henceforth, the Jew is summoned uniquely to reside. Auschwitz
seems at once irreducible to any effort of thought, and
bound to master any attempt at thought. The former religious certainties are no longer valid, but the revelation
continues with the modern assertion of a transcendence
that has a pure secularized horizon. By the ordeal of annihilation, the Jew finds himself the guardian of that opening
up to "authentic existence" that Heidegger called for and
that joins biblical obligation to life. But, henceforth,
because of the Holocaust, this projection will always
remain fragmentary and incomplete—which is true, also,
in Fackenheim's opinion, for the State of Israel.

In Praise of
Mystery

I can grasp in a profound way, and from within, this
mental process that looks for a rationality of the world in
its divine necessity. And I can understand these anguished
thinkers who have sought to tame the Shoah. I will even
say, and I will have occasion to come back to this, that, to
a certain extent, my intellectual guides in Islam, the ones

I chose during de-colonialization and the emergence of Arab-Islamism, disappointed me when they seemed to me to pass over the astounding singularity of Jewish history and the specificity of its survival. If there is a story that can topple into the sacred or the mystical dramatically, it is certainly the Jewish one.

One would have to lack all sense of the epic or, as Malraux said, any "cosmic antenna" not to feel concerned by the Jewish mystery—at least as much as by the miracle of Greece. Let us emphasize in passing that, for me, the word "mystery" is the key word. Insofar as we try to subdue, to reduce, that is to say to impoverish this mystery with a definition, then the clarities we discover in it become unacceptable for me. The necessity (the obligation) to respect and preserve the mystery of the Holocaust cannot take the form of renouncing elucidation of the conditions from which it arose. The important thing is that we not try to make the exceptional or unique commonplace in the course of elaborating a doctrine of barbarism that we should study in order to keep it from occurring again in the centuries to come.

Eichmann in Jerusalem   The fact remains that as time passed, a specifically Jewish memory centered on the genocide would develop every-where, as Peter Novick analyzes it in an important work,

the Jewish Prison
Jean Daniel

The Holocaust in American Life. The process he describes,
the different stages that he identifies, are equally valid for
France, Germany, and Israel. First came World War II,
during which the specific fate of the Jews is not perceived
as such—the struggle was against the German invader, not
against the exterminator of the Jews. (Many of the Free
French, however, would react that way in the ranks of the
Leclerc army.) Then the post-war silence came, which
wouldn't really be broken until 1961, with the Eichmann
trial. Novick writes that "the Eichmann trial was the first
time that the American public was presented with the
Holocaust as a distinct—and distinctively Jewish—entity."[3]
By the American public—but also by the rest of the world,
that is how Ben-Gurion's intentions were perceived. Then
came the Six Days War (1967) and the Yom Kippur War
(1973) that marked a reorientation in the Jewish
consciousness towards the obsessive summons to the
duty of remembering.

Things became incredibly weighed down with
ambiguities when the State of Israel decided to organize
Eichmann's trial. Why did the trial of this killer, this executioner of Jews, of Jewish populations—my phrase is the fruit
of a semantic decision: I'm not speaking of people but of
populations—take place in Jerusalem, capital of a State that
had been rediscovered after more than two thousand years?
When it took place, objections, to my great surprise, were

---

[3] Peter Novick, *The Holocaust in American Life* (Boston and New York:
Houghton Mifflin, 1999), p. 134.

scarce, even if reservations formulated by Karl Jaspers had
to be dealt with. In a letter addressed to Hannah Arendt,
who went to Jerusalem in December 1960 to follow the trial
for the *New Yorker*, the German philosopher observed that
"Israel didn't even exist when the murders were committed.
Israel is not the Jewish people.... The Jewish people are
more than the state of Israel, not identical with it. If Israel
were lost, the Jewish people would still not be lost. Israel
does not have the right to speak for the Jewish people as a
whole."[4] To which Hannah Arendt replied: "Israel may not
have the right to speak for the Jews of the world. (Although
I'd like to know who really does have the right to speak for
the Jews qua Jews in a political sense. Certainly, many Jews
don't want to be represented as Jews or only want to be in a
religious sense. So Israel has no right to speak for them. But
what about the others? Israel is the only political entity we
have. I don't particularly like it, but there's not much I can
do about that.) But in any case Israel has the right to speak
for the victims, because the large majority of them (300,000)
are living in Israel now as citizens. The trial will take place
in the county in which the injured parties and those who
happened to survive are. You say that Israel didn't exist
then. But one could say that it was for the sake of these victims that Palestine became Israel."[5]

As the historian Henry Rousso recalls, "Israel in the
first place constructed itself against the image of the Jew

---

[4] Hannah Arendt and Karl Jaspers, *Correspondence 1926-1969*, edited by Lotte Kohler
and Hans Saner, translated by Robert and Rita Kimber (New York: Harcourt Brace
Javanovich, 1992), pp. 410-411.

[5] Ibid., p. 415.

the Jewish Prison
Jean Daniel

as victim." The historian observes that it was the "young Israelis brought up on a new military tradition, and discovering, incredulous, through the Eichmann trial, the incredible Nazi machinery" who posed the question of the supposed "passivity" of the Jews faced with Nazism.

Let us also recall with Hannah Arendt that Ben-Gurion never truly realized all the ramifications of genocide to the point of seeing in National Socialism the salutary shock that would provoke a great wave of Jewish migration to Palestine. Let us again remember Hannah Arendt's anxiety in seeing the Eichmann trial transformed by the Zionist leader into a weapon of propaganda aiming, in effect, to prove, to the entire world, that "a Jew [can] only live honorably and in complete security in Israel." Because of this, the Eichmann trial marks a turning point.

Memory and
History

The Hebrew State intended, from then on, to take charge of the memory of all Jewish populations, of all the diasporas. Zionist historicism would consist, as Saul Friedlander has pointed out, in integrating Auschwitz "into the historical sequence of Jewish catastrophes leading to the redemptive birth of a Jewish State," and Israel would appropriate the massacre of the Jews and make of it, says Henry Rousso, "an element of political legitimization."

With this new claim to becoming the guardian of the memory of genocide, the link is made between Israel (hence Zionism) and the whole community of Jews. From that moment forward, we have to do with a State like all the others that claims to manage the memory of a people that is not like any other. Starting from this conflicting dialectic, the young State would have a tendency to act on several different levels. When it conducts itself as a State should, they talk about interests of state; if it deviates from behavior condoned by other states or by universal law, it invokes that memory of which it is the custodian. Certainly, its great difficulty will be to convince its neighbors, its rivals, its partners of this. How could victims see their executioners as other victims? But that is essential. Edward Said, a Palestinian Christian writer, who died in New York on September 25, 2003, and who for a long time had a large readership and genuine prestige in Muslim Palestinian circles, taught his people a lesson one day, in an article appearing in the *New York Review of Books* (and reprinted in *Le Monde diplomatique*). He said to them: If you do not try to understand them (speaking of the Jews), how can you expect them to understand us?

The controversy would turn out to be a major one, sometimes a passionate one. Paul Ricoeur for example was reproached for making himself the historiographer of barbarism, a reproach that conferred on him, without his wishing it, an ideological dignity—thus betraying the *duty of memory*. This was absolutely unfair, and his protests against this accusation were meticulously appropriate. The Protestant metaphysician, very close to the Jewish Levinas, still had difficulty denying the conflict between the memory of the genocide as crime and its history as event. To accept one at the expense of the other is to end up making the crime sacred and giving it a religious dimension.

*From the
"Passion"
to the War*

It is Levinas, as we've seen, who, whether out of conviction or for apologetical purposes, uses the Christian term "Passion" when he speaks of Israel's "Passion," referring to the genocide. But the Christian Passion was the way to Redemption and salvation! Posed, imposed, crushing, the question remains: What is the meaning of the Shoah? How can we think after Auschwitz? If there is no more meaning, what should we make of the idea of God? And how can we acknowledge the fact that the shrines are filling up? Should we continue going to Temple to worship the Eternal? To love Him? To fear Him? But to do that is, in a roundabout way, to give back meaning to things! It is to accuse oneself, to repent, to accept the fact that we may have deserved it, by having been unfaithful to the Covenant, to the Law, to the contract, to all the promises that the spouses of God committed themselves to on Sinai. And where does the idea come from, that the Jews ever deserved that? What did they do but give beacons to humanity and make up the leaven of nations? What did they do to be persecuted? And in the name of what masochism could a spectacular and scandalous self-flagellation absolve God? Isn't that a manifestation evocative of Jeremiah where one expects a revolt evoking Job? God never replied in a convincing way to Job, though the literary quality of this reply reaches lofty heights. And Job finally made do with a sublime but despotic poem after having been one of the greatest rebels of mankind, along with Prometheus and Daedelus.

In any case, the cult of memory of five million Jews—six, five, four, what difference does it make?— organized itself throughout the West. Memory of scandalous martyrdom, or of a punishment deserved? Until that date in 1967, those six days, more famous than any, when Israel (the State, this time) waged a war led by Jews in the name of Jews, and won it. Then they reconciled themselves with God. They stopped repenting. If they were victorious, it was because He had wanted them to be so. In short, He had punished us when we were peaceful. He protected us when we were warriors. Germany razed to the ground: worse than the ten plagues of Egypt! Israel at the summit of its splendor: better than, or as good as, the first Temple!

Does the terrible Shoah have a hidden and beneficial meaning, then? That is how certain devout, unconditional supporters of the Jewish State ended up seeing it, without admitting it, even to themselves.

IV.
Israel as Will and as Representation

Then answered the Lord unto Job out of the
whirlwind, and said, ...
Wilt thou also disannul my judgment?
wilt thou condemn me,
that thou mayest be righteous?

Job 40:6,8.

In the beginning, in 1948, things were not simple. We were living in a period of anti-colonialism. And this in fact was the springboard and the *raison d'être* for the Left in the West as well as for the Left in the turbulent Third World.

In 1956, I went to Israel for the first time, and I returned full of enthusiasm from my discovery of the *kibbutzim*. They were the great dream of the pioneers of the Left. I had at the time already been active and written on behalf of the Algerians and the Tunisians, since I advocated for the policies of Pierre Mendès France in Tunisian independence. Strangely, though, at the time—a proof of how difficult it is to reconstruct those days—no one was surprised at my writing such lengthy and positive articles about Israel, at a time when they were just asides to my anti-colonialist campaign on the side of Arabs and Muslims.

And then, as I've recounted in *Voyage au bout de la nation* (Journey to the end of the nation), one day, the Algerian leader, Ben Bella, who had made me his friend, brought me along on his first trip to Cairo, a journey that mattered enormously to him. In the plane, as we were flying over desert, he said to me: "I wanted Nasser to win in Suez, and he won; I wanted the independence of Algeria, I got it, and now all that's left is the liberation of Palestine." I said to him, "Look at these deserts, don't you think there's room for everyone?" His answer: "In a desert there's always room! My nanny was Jewish. That has nothing to do with it, but in Palestine, that's different. They're foreigners."

That is how I discovered the problem of Israel. My discovery of Zionism was abruptly accompanied by the hatred it provoked. I had a sympathy, even a feeling of complicity, for these Muslim victims of colonialism, but when they uttered this kind of statement, it not only offended me but worried me.

In fact, for my part, during that whole period of anti-colonialism, I foolishly hoped, or fixated on the illusion, that Maghrebi nationalism—less affected than the other Arab nationalisms, more distanced than they from the theaters of operation, better prepared to understand the Western point of view on the ambiguity of Israel, and that, finally, often revealed itself to be extremely stubborn in dealing with the Arab League—would contribute a note of openness and ecumenical hope. I was counting then on the Tunisians, the Moroccans, the Algerians. Nor was I alone in that. At *Les Temps Modernes* (the journal founded in 1945 by Sartre and Simone de Beauvoir), for instance,

Israel as Will and
as Representation

there were vigilant friends of Israel who took sides against the war in Algeria—Sartre himself, and Claude Lanzmann—and there were even real Zionists. I also remember that, during the negotiations at Évian with the FLN (the Algerian Front de Libération Nationale), the Socialist Gaston Defferre published, in *Le Monde*, an editorial in which he implored the future leaders of the Algerian government to show "benevolence and realism" towards the young Jewish State. In Cairo, one day, visiting the leaders of the Algerian revolution who had gathered there, I put forward the idea to Ferhat Abbas that the Israelis and the Algerians had many points in common: They had gone from terrorism to resistance, from resistance to revolution; they had to construct a State that had vanished, one for two millennia, the other for a few centuries. Ferhat Abbas reacted only with a smile, probably not wanting to disappoint someone useful to his plans at the time, deferring till later the manifestation of his hostility to Israel.

Once again, it was the time when Israel did not seem militarily invincible, when Israel was withdrawn inside exacting borders that were difficult to defend, and asked only to be "recognized." Neither Jerusalem nor the West Bank were part of its territory. The Israeli cause was perfectly justifiable. The intransigence of the Arab refusal, however, was open to question.

the Jewish Prison
Jean Daniel

In Search of
Legitimacy

Soon I would come to protest that the concept of colonialism was ambiguous. I refused to liken the Jewish State to a form of colonization. If we ask about violence, no nation was born without recourse to it. As to the exploitation of "natives," that was nonexistent in Israel, since the Israelis cultivated their lands themselves, and Arab workers were volunteers who were in the minority at the time. Finally, the actuality of a Palestinian nation was not evident when the Jewish pioneers arrived. I have long been aware of the fact that Palestinian nationalism was born, and developed, thanks to the Israelis. Arabs don't like to be reminded of this. Nonetheless, there are some exceptions, notably the representative in Paris of the PLO, Leila Shahid, who readily confirms this.

I asserted that there was the unquestionable *right* of the Palestinians and the inescapable *fact* of the Israelis. The antiquity of the Arab population was obvious, and the ethnic link with neighboring populations was inarguable. When the United Nations recognized the Israeli State and decided on partition, they granted, by a very large majority— let us recall though that there were not yet any representatives of the ex-colonial countries, which would perhaps have changed the vote—legality to the State of Israel. But it then was up to Israel to move from legality to legitimacy. And I thought that legitimacy would be won for Israel when *de facto* became *de jure* by virtue of the intensity of its sacrifices and by being recognized by other nations.

Israel as Will and
as Representation

I had a strong suspicion that I was searching for compromises with my ideal principles. But I had decided to fight for these compromises, because I was struck by the absurdity of a conflict so ridiculously territorial. In any case, for the Jews of Israel, I was ready to plead guilty, but only on condition that I would refuse in advance any calling into question of a State legalized by UN recognition in 1948.

The Turning-
Point of 1967

One single phenomenon, but one with many different and peculiar aspects that are sometimes hard to interpret, has been the cause of a veritable transformation of the "Jewish soul"—this time I do not hesitate to use an expression that, elsewhere, I object to, as we shall see. This phenomenon is the war of 1967 (from which the Israelis emerged victorious) and its consequences—incalculable for the young Hebrew State, for the Palestinians, the Arabs, and all of the Near East, but also for the Jews in the four corners of the world, especially in Europe and France, and in fact for the world itself.

In the first place, the Israeli victory strengthened the ties between the new Jerusalem and the diaspora. It revived Judaism in places that had been de-Judaicized or, as we try not to say today, "assimilated." It fostered a major return to the religious and the spiritual. It is difficult to see how the Jews remained sheltered from the immense movements of thought, really great tidal waves of thought, which led humanity to the temptation of turning away from Reason for the sake of the Spirit, and from philosophies of History for the sake of morality. This is not the place to ponder the mishaps of Reason even if, in passing, I can take the opportunity to attack all unconditional appeals to religions in excusing behavior we would deny to ideologies.

What is most distressing of all is that such regressions are accepted by respectable, serious thinkers in the name of the celebrated affirmation of identity. Like all my contemporaries, I followed the path that went in search of our roots. I felt the need of doing this strongly enough to make it the subject of a book, *Voyage au bout de la nation*. But despite all that, I cannot accept all the stupidities that have been written, and all the crimes that have been committed, in the name of that identity. First of all, what is at stake? What kind of identity are we dealing with? One that evokes the famous question: "Tell me what your country, your family, is, tell me what your law is?" How can one decide what defines a people? And who would presume to do so? We need to recall at this point that History and identity are reconstituted myths. The former is nothing other than poetry, as Paul Valéry said. The latter, for Jean-Pierre Vernant, is only a variable and utilitarian construction.

Israel as Will and
as Representation

Centrality of
the Land?

Today, the idea that belonging to the land of *Eretz Israel* and to the State of Israel constitutes an essential component of Jewishness is disseminated as an obvious fact. Not a component of religion, or of hope for a messiah, or of a branch of Judaism, but of the very fact of Jewish existence and being. It is only because of this assertion, established as a dogma, that we confuse anti-Zionism with anti-Semitism, that any questioning of the citizens of the Israeli state becomes an insult to the peoples of the diaspora, and that we assign particular but completely complementary functions to Jews who live in Israel and to those who live in "exile." Each Jew is enjoined to feel and demonstrate solidarity with a government other than the one in which he has chosen to spend his life, and with which he can at times be in conflict.

This involves the question of an innovation that occurred long after the destruction of the second Temple, and this innovation is enormous. For more than two thousand years, the Jews did not think to link their fate with that of a land, much less a State. Of course religious Jews intoned hopes in their prayers to live "next year in Jerusalem." Of course they dreamed, sometimes, of making a sort of pilgrimage there, to a land that was holy only because it allowed one to practice holiness there. The splendor of the kingdoms of Judea and of the legends that accompany it certainly inspired dreams. Certainly we can read in the Babylonian Talmud that "one who has no land is not a man," but the idea that the Jewish destiny could be accomplished only in Israel, as natural as it seems to have become today, was almost aberrant before the birth of the State of Israel, even before the victories of 1967 and the reunification of Jerusalem.

In fact, as Georges Bensoussan reports in his *Histoire politique et intellectuelle du sionisme* (Political and intellectual history of Zionism), "according to a tradition of medieval Judaism, the holiness of the land of Israel demands a high level of spirituality of its inhabitants. For this land is not the place of just any people; it is the land inhabited by God, the natural place of virtue, the residence of the Eternal." And Maimonides, in his *Book of Commandments*, does not make the obligation to reside in the Holy Land one of the 613 fundamental prescriptions of Jewish Law. Only study of the Torah matters; love of the land is secondary.

We have seen that, from the beginning, the creation *ex nihilo* of the Jewish people and its Election were accompanied by the promise of the Covenant made by God to establish the chosen people in a chosen land. From "the beginning," God promised a land, and one that was called "promised." But before we speculate about the function of a territorial space and about the role its inhabitants should play in it, we should note that ignoring this promise for two

Israel as Will and
as Representation

thousand years gave others, in this instance the Arabs, a
chance to take root in the land for such a long period that
it amounts to legitimate appropriation. We should then
note that it was not in memory of the promise that the State
of Israel was created. And this is a good time to emphasize
the fact that what they use to make a law today was only a
possibility yesterday.

Rabbis and   At the beginnings of Zionism, some people wanted to
Zionists   create a State just like others anywhere in the world. Most
of the preliminary drafts, in fact, do not distinguish
between the land of Israel and any other territory. Some
Zionists, actually wishing to free themselves from
Judaism, from the "religious burden" it represents, and
impatient to build a secular society, went so far as to
exclude the idea of settling in Israel. Others wanted only
to rediscover or invent roots for themselves. Passionate
and impassioned debates thus centered on the great questions about the function of an Israeli territory. But, let me
repeat it, one cannot transform what had only been a
circumstantial opportunity constructed by History and
provided by Providence into an absolute of identity. There
were even religious groups who thought that God could not
have offered a land where one had to do anything but pray
in praise of His power and His qualities.

the Jewish Prison
Jean Daniel

Some even became the denigrators of any demand for a national existence for the Jewish people. Thus the rabbi of Vienna, Moritz Guedemann, accused Zionism of bringing the Jewish faith down to the dimensions of a simple particularism, of reducing Judaism to a national fact when it should be devoted to the universal. For him, Zionism represents a "spiritual regression": Thanks to the rejection of violence and bloodshed inscribed in the heart of Judaism, the Jews had saved themselves from sinking into nationalist ideology. The continuity of the Jewish people came precisely from the fact that it had always held itself apart, and had always privileged humanity over occupying territory, the universal over the particular.

The Hesitation of Herzl

In his book, Theodor Herzl did not come to a decision about the question of whether the return to Zion was vital or not. For many years, the question remained. The urgency, for Herzl but also for Pinsker, was to obtain some territory: "Possibility that the Holy Land could become our own land. This would be all the better. But it is not the essential thing," the author of *Auto-Emancipation* writes; "it is a question, above all, of examining where the country is that is able to offer Jews of every provenance, forced to leave their native country, the possibility of entry and refuge." During the first Zionist Congress that took place in Basel in

Israel as Will and
as Representation

1897, with Herzl presiding, the exclusive supporters of the land of Israel and those who were called "territorialists," for whom the question mattered little, confronted each other. By the end of the congress, however, everyone agreed on the choice of Palestine as the place of Jewish settlement.

The sense of agreement was only temporary, however, since in 1903 the question arose again after the pogroms recently perpetrated in Russia. The minister for the British Colonies, fearing a new wave of Jewish immigrants, suggested Uganda to Herzl. Those faithful to Zion were vehemently opposed to the supporters of the African solution. Herzl seemed favorable to Uganda but only as a stage on the path leading to Jerusalem. The stakes are large: Is it a matter of reconstructing Zion, or rather making a State of Jews, a State for the Jews?

The question was formulated that way, and, when it was resolved, it was with the idea, in effect, that it was difficult to create a purely negative home, born from persecution by others, and with the sole mission of assuming control of one's fate. At that very important time—for the best minds, throughout the century, kept stressing a parallel between Israel and the United States—the founders rallied round a plan that was contrary to that of America. The majority of the Zionist Congress adopted the idea of resettling Zion. They relied on a twofold legitimacy, one linked to response to persecution, the other to fidelity to roots. This attitude was opposite to that of the American pioneers. Why? Because the Pilgrim Fathers had the ambition of creating something absolutely new. They set out to conquer the New World. The Israelis, though, were not building the new land. They were exhuming the old dream.

From Isolation to Regeneration But if we consent to the notion that there can be no feeling of national belonging without taking root somewhere, then isn't there some necessity for the Jews to settle in Palestine? Where can the Jewish people satisfy its need for roots if not on the land spoken of in the Torah and the rest of the Bible? That is the question, in the form of an objection, that sets Georges Bensoussan against the Zionist territorialists. Objectively taking stock of all the contradictory positions of this great debate, he still couldn't keep from reproaching Pinsker, or Herzl, with underestimating the power of the special link that ties the Jews to the land of Israel and failing to recognize "the central role played by the land of Israel in the imagination of the Jewish people." Another land would not evoke anything. Though Herzl was "competent on the question of the State," Bensoussan concludes, obviously he "was less so on that of the nation."

Zéev (Vladimir) Jabotinsky would eventually make himself the systematic theoretician of this idea of "nationality." At the Zionist Congress, he described himself as the

Israel as Will and
as Representation

defender of the doctrine of "splendid isolation," which gave rise to an animated discussion with Theodor Herzl. Jabotinsky, who was to die as a refugee in New York in 1940, developed a concept of Zionism that assumes difference, brandishes isolation, and even welcomes persecution. Jabotinsky was of the opinion that the mission the Jews were entrusted with, the mission to which they had to bear witness within this land and not in the diaspora, could be fulfilled only through unpopularity, even hostility. Not only did we know we would be hated by everyone, but we had to be. It is within this identity-forming hostility that we would become ourselves.

The objective of the founders of the State of Israel, however, would at first be to make themselves accepted by others. Ben-Gurion said, "We will not be a State like the others, with neighbors who do not acknowledge our existence." Jabotinsky, in advance, said no—and his disciple today could well be Ariel Sharon, although Sharon claims to be faithful to Ben-Gurion. There is a sort of incomprehensible compromise between the supposed universality of the Jewish message, which we believed to be indisputable, and the brandished exclusivity of the Jewish Election that can be realized only in the glory of conquest or the suffering of a curse.

Jabotinsky's life was marked by the three major events that marked the existence of Israel: secession, armed struggle, concrete symbols of identity. All of Jabotinsky's theories and actions, substituting revolutionary action for the logic of law, reflect one single imperative: the immediate advent of a Jewish State in *Eretz Israel* by means of war. But, at the same time, this absolutist activist continued to be a man of letters: He was one of the first translators of the great works of humanity into modern Hebrew. With Jabotinsky arises the idea that Israeli identity must also form a culture that defines itself against, among other things, the Jewish inheritance of the diaspora.

Many complex motives are involved here. On the one hand, Zionism proposes rebellion against the exile's state of humiliation. The armed Israeli erases the memory of the subjected, victimized Jew. The Jew is in fact "regenerated" according to that progressive myth of the New Man widespread throughout all activist milieus in the nineteenth century. The cultural antagonism that arose from this was marked by Israeli anxiety about the Shoah until the 1960's (the Eichmann trial) and the diasporic anxiety about Israel until 1967 (the Six Days War). It was overcome, to the benefit of Zionism, after the 1970's, when it gave way to the dominant vision of today, that is, the feeling of having revived a "sacred History" or the "Election." On the other hand, for the Israeli to be truly the "regenerated" Jew, re-settlement in the "Promised Land" turned out to be indispensable, so that the condition of diaspora seemed

Israel as Will and
as Representation

only like a digression between independence lost and independence regained. Against the progressive myth of regeneration, leaning towards the future, the Bible offers a genealogical myth of the golden age, making the past more dynamic. The result of all this is the centrality of the Holy Land, whose reappropriation becomes the condition for regeneration. The conservative, revolutionary, and authoritarian vision of Jabotinsky, dangerous as it may seem on the present Israeli scene, nonetheless shaped the way people think today.

On Philosopher-
Prophets

In quite a different way Martin Buber develops the idea that there exists an inextricable link between the mission with which the Jewish people were entrusted and the land of Israel. Only on the land of their ancestors can Jews accomplish the moral mission that was entrusted to them, but this land can be qualified as ancestral only if it becomes the setting for their moral mission. "At no moment in the history of Israel," he writes in 1944, "has the country been the exclusive property of the People; ownership has always been accompanied by the requirement to make it what God wanted it to be. That is how the special link between this People and this land is marked, from the start, by what the land must be, what must be done in it, what must be accomplished there. The People is incapable of accomplishing its mission without its land, and the land cannot accomplish it without this people: Only the link of mutual faith can lead them there." Both the people and the land were chosen, he writes in *On Zion: The History of an Idea.*

The settling of the Jews in Palestine has meaning and legitimacy only if they take on the task of building a fairer society, offering themselves in that way as a model for the rest of humanity, opening the way to a world of greater justice. The Jewish State must be a *State of witness* according to Buber's phrase, written just after the terrible carnage that was the First World War. That is why Buber can assert, without contradiction, that "historical right" is a chimera, that the right of the Jews does not have its source in some historical anteriority. The fact remains that Buber never stopped warning the Jews of a nationalist drift within Zionism. The obsession with normalization carries along with it the risk of succumbing to an idolatry of the nation-state.

In the same lineage as this prophetic resistance of Jewish philosophers, Emmanuel Levinas showed himself even more mistrustful of this yearning to take root and its possible outcomes. All the more so since this notion seemed to him particularly foreign to Judaism. "Judaism has always been free with regard to places." For "freedom with respect to sedentary forms of existence is, perhaps, the human way of existing in the world.... This [Jewish]

freedom considers the value of settling down to be of
secondary importance and establishes other forms of
fidelity and responsibility" that are no less strong.
Nothing, for Levinas, is more dangerous than the "genius
of Place," this genius that seduces us and makes us prefer
landscapes and architectures to another human face. This
genius links us to "all those heavy, sedentary things we are
tempted to prefer to man." As Alain Finkielkraut recalls,
Levinas kept questioning "those Israelis and Zionists who
confuse Zionism with some sort of mystique about land as
territory." But just as contradictory as all the others,
Levinas asserted—as we have seen earlier—that after the
Shoah, Israel needed a nation-state, one that could be
nowhere else but in Palestine.

*Haunting
Aporias*

Now the concept of Election reappears, all the more
ambiguous and dangerous since it involves that of a
Covenant, which implies an obligation for Israel to settle in
a foreign land. In effect, as soon as it is a question of the
supposedly inextricable link between the people of Israel
and its land, and even of the supposed incapacity of
Judaism to flourish outside of Israel—so agonizing for
some of the prophets—it becomes very difficult to shift,
adjust, and distinguish between a blessing bestowed and a
virtue to be earned. Either the community is comprised of

a people among other peoples, a nation among other nations, both acknowledged by the surrounding communities, or it is a question of a gathering of Jews within a State that has, let us repeat, reasons of State, secrets of State, an army, a diplomacy, borders to defend, an ethnic purity to safeguard—then the State is, by definition, unable to be faithful to Election.

The Israelis can indeed be in accord about the Bible as an index of identity. But as soon as they confuse the spiritual with the temporal, as in Islam, then they can only find the most blatant contradictions in the sacred texts. Everything and its opposite can be found there. A godsend, for arguments between scholars of the Law. One day when I was confiding my frustrations to the Hellenist Jean-Pierre Vernant, he replied that all men—following the example of "his" Greeks—seek in their past not so much for an affirmation of identity as for a collective mythology. What we call our roots is often only the intensity of common beliefs. Because they are intense, because they are common, they are endowed with a strength that we feel nostalgic for, and that we would like to recover.

If, from this perspective, the Israelis seek, consciously or not, only a mythology useful to their aim, then, in effect, they have to come to a decision, as do we. What mythology? From what time? A mythology for a country like all others, or for the chosen people? Election for the great Israel of the God of Hosts, or the mission of a people that is sometimes wandering, sometimes settled, but always and endlessly witnesses of the universal? Can one make innocent people pay the price for the most terrible persecution since the birth of the world? And do the newly persecuted, the new victims, become, in their turn, witnesses against Israel? Or, on the contrary, should the survivors of genocide, and their descendants, transform themselves into protesters mobilized against all violence, wherever it appears, whoever its perpetrators are, even and especially if the victims of that violence are not Jewish? Shouldn't the real message of the genocide that those who have escaped it proclaim be, along with the Book, "If violence answers violence, when will violence stop"?

*De-Judaizing
According to
Joshua*

This is a terrible contradiction, to make a gift of a land while still demanding exemplarity. The invention of the territorial taking root of the promise is an appalling thing. God Himself finds this taking root risky. He says to Israel, "I am going to *lend* you this land." You will note that this people of priests and witnesses is led by Joshua. The prophecy is granted to Moses, but realization of it is granted to Joshua. Joshua is a warrior, a warlord; he will conquer the land of Canaan. He conducts himself neither as a witness nor as a priest, but as a warlord. One begins to wonder if the original de-Judaizing really began with Joshua.

Almost all the problems concerning the survival of the State of Israel revolve around the use of violence, its justification, its frequency, its consequences. That is of course the business of every State, especially of every young State. No doubt about it. We might even say that all revolutionary countries have to confront the problems of the goal and the means to it, of betraying principles to preserve existence, or denying freedom to enemies of freedom. On the one hand, it is difficult to see how we can permit a State like Israel to do what we now no longer permit to States that once defined themselves as "revolutionary." On the other hand, insofar as this State claims not only to recover a homeland it lost two thousand years ago (which is already highly debatable), but also to settle in the land of the Bible in order to continue to bear witness to the biblical message, then we are quite right to expect more of it than it seems to expect of itself. As Pierre Vidal-Naquet says, "The paradox of Israel is that it is both the accomplishment of a dream of normalization—having finally, like other countries, customs inspectors, prisons, and judges to fill these prisons—and the embodiment of a very old Messianism that aims to create a righteous city. I myself feel this keenly, and, to give a clear example, an Israeli torturer... makes me more indignant than a

French torturer." The State of Israel is a State, and we will
never stop defining it as such. But we must know what a
State is, we must reread what Hegel writes about this. A
State is a cold monster that has no allies and has only
interests. This State, because it is a State, is like all
others. Israel cannot, at one and the same time, ask to be
treated like all countries at war or in conflict, and then
differently from all the other countries.

*Cause Against
Cause*
Let us remember: To be hero and saint at the same time,
that is the only meaning of Election. In the *kibbutzim*, in
the pioneers' day, non-believers were persuaded of this.
There was a proud affirmation of a feeling that one had
constantly to deserve the rediscovered land to assure the
emergence of new Jews. How did this feeling disappear?
First of all through the inheritance of a Western, socialist
arrogance. Some of the founders of Israel thought of themselves as being in the vanguard of Western civilization.
They believed they were fulfilling the values of progress
and justice. One can see traces of this stupefying complacency in more than one official document—and in the
analysis of many actions, such as announcing that the
Arabs could only benefit from the return of Jews to
the country of their ancestors. For they too could thus
discover their own fallen or lost civilization.

the Jewish Prison
Jean Daniel

All this was not to reckon with a number of factors, including that of religion. I have been reproached for "psychologizing" or even "spiritualizing" my approach to the Israeli-Arab conflict. I have wanted here in effect to relativize (without denying) any intervention of the economic or the strategic in aid of the religious.

The emptying of the religious was certainly a widespread reaction in rationalist milieus at the end of the twentieth century. It is what has often, as I have shown, led outside commentators to reduce the Jewish destiny to a collection of reactions against anti-Semitism. In the same way they explained the famous "Arab refusal"—constantly opposing the Israelis, and so admirably defined, from its beginning, by Maxime Rodinson—as the sole will of the native people of Palestine to struggle against dispossession from their land. This recourse to the rational did not succeed without some feeling of uneasiness, since the Israelis spiritualized the choice of the place of their settlement, while in reaction the Arabs did not hesitate to inveigh against these infidels against whom they thought a holy war was justified.

We told ourselves that the survivors of the death camps had recourse to History only in order to legitimize their young State. To dignify this discovered land, they had to declare it as rediscovered. As to the Arabs, their racism could only be situational and adventitious: It had no historical significance. Moreover, each of these things was true in its own case. But the explanation of it was sadly incomplete. It was like this, but it was not only like this, or we needed it to be not only like this. We resign ourselves poorly, Tocqueville observes, to the plurality of causes in history. Passions need a single object on which to fixate. That was truer here than elsewhere. We could not impute to chance the Israeli plan to create in Palestine first a refuge-State and then, as if goaded on by the Arab refusal, to establish *Eretz Israel*, the Greater Israel. We could not attribute to self-defense alone this gathering together of Arabs prompted by Israeli violence, for which a precedent was suddenly found in the sacred.

The Reversal We should accept the idea that Zionism is a movement of liberation that was perceived as an act of colonization. Here it is not a question of opinion. And especially not of a subjective or partisan interpretation of the verdicts of History. It is simply a question of observing, as we do in marital conflicts, the radical differences of real-life experiences in each side's intense sincerity.

A Jew who has escaped the ghettos and the camps, and who sees himself caught up, magnetized, by the land of legend and of his original myths, could experience the incredible adventure only as an emancipation determined by some higher power. This is true whether he is a believer or not—and in any case non-believing Jews seem to act essentially just like religious Jews, since both are

the Jewish Prison
Jean Daniel

conceived of as belonging to Judaism. In a more or less
obscure way, both can find links with Election and with its
territorial roots in *Eretz Israel*.

It just so happens that this movement, which has its
origins in the Nazi inferno and its future in a homecoming
to the Promised Land, turns out to be one of the most ordinary and prosaic stages in the typical process of colonization. As supporters and privileged heralds of the European
genius, the Jewish pioneers in Israel were obviously filled
with a vision, at its worst conquering and at its best protective, of the colonized or colonizable peoples. Still we
should point out that their attitude, in a foreign country,
was closer to British indifference than to the pedagogical
utopia of French colonialism.

The Jews did not feel they were invested with any
mission with respect to any particular group: They had
enough to handle with the construction of their State and the
definition of their identity. They were received not only as
allies of the colonial powers, but also as elements that
despite their attachment to the Book could scarcely be more
alien to the Arabian subcontinent and to its Islamic religion.

No one would recover from this initial tragedy. The
Jews have never acknowledged a colonial situation. The
Arabs never saw them as anything but colonists. From a
strictly legal point of view, the plan of partition determined
in 1947 by the UN put an end to the colonized-colonizer

relationship. Two sovereign countries. Two peoples, equal. Neither conquest nor domination. Nothing that could be expected to arise from the usual colonial phenomenon.

Thenceforth, the Jews were justified in brandishing a good conscience, as Israeli citizens welcomed and recognized by the international community. They still needed to be accepted by their neighbors. The fact of being refused by their neighbors led them to become once again Jews like all the others, whereas they had wanted to succeed at being Israelis.

*Propaganda
and
Barbarism*

So after all this, should Zionism be located within the vast colonial enterprise of the West and its global market? Some carried this attitude to a radical extreme whose excesses were too ostentatious not to be suspected. The simplistic accusations of those who describe American imperialists manipulating Zionist puppets and putting survivors of the death camps in the heart of the Arab world as Trojan horses of international capitalism—such oversimplification has to surmount too many objections.

Great Britain's opposition to the formation of the Hebrew State? An accident. Roosevelt's disavowal? A diversion. Spain's hostility? Mere chance. As to the decisive support of the Soviet Union and Czechoslovakia for the founders of the Jewish State, they refused to recall this. In short, all the loose ends, all the flaws that jutted out of the Procrustes' bed of anti-colonialist comforts were quickly trimmed. They tried to remove the Jewish dimension from the Israeli reality, and the Arab-Islamic dimension from the Palestinian reality.

Aware that we seemed to require these mutilations, the protagonists of the drama set themselves to bringing about things that would nourish a cause in conformity with our expectations. In fact, this was especially the case of the Arabs and the Palestinians, who, because of the humiliation of their successive defeats, produced a revolution within the revolution. The Israelis, for their part, contented themselves with raking in the fruits of their victories before becoming prisoners of them.

The advent of the PLO, the Palestinian Liberation Organization, was in a way as considerable as the birth of the Viet-minh, the Cuban *barbudos*, and the Algerian FLN. These are, or were, movements that created myths with no relation to their original reality, their initial importance. Arab nationalism, under its Nasserian form, had found in the first humiliation inflicted by Israel something to nourish a veritable doctrine of rebirth. *The Philosophy of the Revolution*, the famous little book by Nasser, was to discover, thanks to misfortune (or rather in the face of misfortune), a possible future for Arab greatness. Such a future was obviously foreshadowed by the golden age of the seventh to the twelfth centuries.

The Nasser nationalism that developed in Cairo, in forms adapted to a country that proposed to play an international role, used as its anti-Israeli propaganda a tainted register, even sometimes a frankly vile one. It was difficult for even the most pro-Arab European or African Leftist to feel personally represented by Egypt's foreign radio broadcasts, *La Voix des Arabes* (The Arab Voice), or by the suggestions, stupefying in their hateful vulgarity, of a leader like the sinister Shukeiry. Tito and Nkrumah, eminences in the club of the unaligned, promptly complained to their friend Nasser of Shukeiry's shocking outrages. It was a time when all of black Africa, or almost all, was pro-Israeli.

*The Golden
Age*

But we should remember that such an era did exist. The tiny size of the young State, the ardor and faith of its founders; the fact that it was surrounded by enemies, and thus under siege; the secular democracy that flourished there despite the religious inspiration of the Constitution; the universal yet prodigiously efficient quality of its military organization; the resurrection of a language that had till then been restricted to liturgy; the efforts of some of its leaders to diversify their international relations—Israel had been the first State to recognize Libya and then Communist China—and the fact that its ally at that time, in an area as critical as the military, was France much more than the United States—all this kept the "progressives" from banishing Israel from the community of nations.

the Jewish Prison
Jean Daniel

Ben-Gurion, the old lion, chatted about Spinoza and
Plato with U Nu, president of Burma. By one of History's
strange antics, one of the most cultivated communities in
the world, suddenly adopting standards that had till then
been foreign to it, came to scorn an Arab-Islamism that
was proving incapable of conquering a handful of Jews
through force or number.

Adopting the harsh judgments of Ibn Khaldun about
the Arabs, the Israelis judged them utterly, and congenital-
ly, incapable of organization, unity, or victory. So that in
1973, after a first resounding success when the Egyptians
were routed and forced back across the Suez Canal, a reas-
sured General Dayan declared, "The Egyptians have
become Arabs again." An ill-advised statement.

In any case, the State of Israel was unusual, particular,
and unclassifiable enough for the blindest Manichaeism to
become uneasy about it. Bourguiba said there had to be
something special in this State for a Third World friend
like Marshal Tito to reject its suppression, even though he
opposed its expansion.

A bold innovator in the decolonialization of his own
country, the Tunisian leader became a rash precursor on
the Palestinian question. In 1965, breaking with the Arab
League, he implored people to let the Palestinians return
freely to the Plan of Partition adopted by the UN in 1948.
His principle and strategy of conquering the West with

its own weapons involved never turning one's back on
international law. Had he been listened to, Bourguiba
would have prevented one of the tragedies of the century.
He would never have tried to get more than was offered,
by waiting for a Bush to succeed a Clinton, or Sharon to
succeed Barak!

King Hassan II of Morocco observed, not without
condescension, that after all one could easily conceive of
a ghetto on the scale of the Arab world. There was a
ghetto in every country, so why couldn't there be a whole
country like a ghetto, with its own name, and why not a
flag too, a ghetto that would be the object of Muslim tolerance and Arab benevolence? Why couldn't we do what
Westerners could not do? There was in King Hassan's
suggestion a sort of aristocratic offhandedness, but also
a blessed memory of the Andalusian golden age, in the
era of the three kings, and the three religions. The memory, too, of the aid that Jewish doctors, merchants,
philosophers, and engineers brought to the Berber
princes. One could expect anything, in this state of
mind, from a little elite State that might bring this same
kind of assistance to a developing Arabia. And of course
the Moroccans, or at least the Berbers, had a chivalrous
respect for men who know how to conquer and die. Now
that the Jews were deciding to conquer and abandon
their former relationship with death, they were becoming

worthy of consideration. In short, the Israelis, to their mind, had legitimized their existence through blood.

The *Revolutionary* *Myth*

The foundation of the PLO with a charter that advocated a secular, democratic Palestine, open to everyone, would give the revolutionary world an opportunity for mythology and general solidarity. No more fanaticism, no more racism: Muslims and Christians—there were many of the latter among the Palestinian leaders—held out their hands to the Jews. It was no longer a question of "throwing them into the sea" or even of excluding them from the Holy Land. The Palestinians were committed to respecting the rights acquired by the Israelis, though a thousand pragmatic problems of this new ecumenical State remained (perhaps willfully) in the shadows; there genuinely was a considerable effort of opening up, of modernizing, of adapting to the new myths of emancipation and third-world revolution.

Above all, there was a kind of taking hold, or taking into account and consideration, of the message of the West. Suddenly it was Israel that was turning into a closed, religious, fanatical, and racist country. We cannot speak of this PLO plan as a sham. The Israelis soon discerned that the PLO's charter constituted their cleverest and most Westernized stratgem—attempting to make Israel disappear as a State, while still claiming to transform and preserve the individual Israelis.

Israel as Will and
as Representation

Since the dream of Israel, according to the indomitable Golda Meir, was for the Jews to have, finally, a region of the world where they would be a majority, the PLO's proposition signified quite simply the destruction of this dream. But now through the Arab masses a current of inner questioning was passing, of which intellectuals and political leaders in Damascus and Baghdad, but also in Tripoli and Algiers, were becoming aware. Nasser had used Israel to try to unify the Arabs into nationalist dignity.

As to the revolutionaries, they believed that the struggle against Israel had to be used to mobilize the masses and overturn the feudal regimes that were in place. One had to pass from nationalism to revolution.

Radicalizations The PLO, under pressure from Algeria, became an important center where the revolutionary future was being prepared. In the Beirut camps, one could see all the young Japanese, Italians, Cubans, and Vietnamese in search of a revolution to come. They are always the same—available, passionate. We saw them in the American universities against the Vietnam War, we saw them demonstrating against the war in Algeria, we saw them in Cuba helping to bring in the cane sugar harvest, and even sometimes in the Israeli kibbutzim where they had gone to practice communal, rural socialism. But now, in the Palestinian camps, with Libyan money, Soviet weapons, and Algerian strategists, they were learning third-worldism and terrorism. It was a shift that would have consequences in Germany, in Japan, and Italy. This third-world form of Marxism came also to influence the leftist youth movements that suddenly plunged into a deadly, desperate form of radicalism. The Red Brigades inherited this powerful phenomenon. In the archaeology of our modern violence, curiously, at a certain point, the Palestinians were a decisive factor. The myth of the PLO was of real magnitude, and without any relationship to its reality.

Myths are mysterious things. I often reread passages from the book by François Furet on the French Revolution, and I am reminded of this. The PLO, just like the Algerian FLN, fits into the great movements of nationalist emancipation, religious revolt, ethnic affirmation. With the ideological trappings of the time, and within the geo-economic context determined by material resources, they form the history of the second half of the twentieth century.

When the PLO made its opening moves, which seemed humanist to the Jews of the world and progressive to the revolutionaries of the West, the extreme French Left, anti-colonialist by vocation, set about radicalizing its anti-Israeli position. Attacked until then from the right as being pro-Arab, since I had always advocated a federation of two sovereign States, Palestinian and Israeli, now that I called the resistance fighters "terrorists," I was soon attacked from the left by those who urged Israel's extermination.

The PSU (Parti socialiste unifié) and the Trotskyites constituted the vanguard—often Jewish—of anti-Zionism. There was no room for compromise with colonialism. Whatever their intentions were, the Israelis were merely Western colonizers foreign to Arab soil. Like all colonialisms, theirs had to be stopped.

Under the Turks, the English, the Jordanians, the revolts were never carried out in the name of the Palestinians. They rose in the name of the Arabs. The Arabs never liked the Palestinians. They saw the Palestinians as agitators who could destabilize their populations and their governments. They would have liked to have won the First World War and to have preserved control over Palestine.

Caught between Pan-Arabism and Zionism, the Palestinians had to assert their national identity, often in a copy-cat way that would only complicate their conflict with Israel. Without offending the Palestinians' ideal, but emphasizing its religious dimension in the general, anthropological sense of the term, one can observe the "imitative" relationship of their nationalism to Zionism, at least in their discourse. It is a relationship that still seems to exemplify the mimetic rivalry analyzed by René Girard. The rise to prominence of certain attitudes seems to confirm this imitation of the Zionist pattern: the feeling of being abandoned by other nations; feeling the risk of extinction; the role of diaspora, the centrality of the land, the primacy of

Jerusalem; the insistence on the right to return; the sacralization of the struggle, via holy sites and sacred texts.

No value judgment can be formed about this mirror-image effect aggravated by the spiral of reciprocal violences. But, added to the primal and mutual denial, it reveals (rather than explains) the inextricable quality of the conflict.

The Six Days   On the other side, it is difficult to understand Israel at all without taking into account how intoxicating the 1967 victory was to the Jews as a whole. A crushing "lightning-quick" victory, broadcast throughout the entire world, the images—epic on one hand, tragic on the other—captured on television. The Sinai, a desert pierced by a great black furrow of corpses, a little like the way the Nile divides the ocher immensity of Egypt; the long line of Arab prisoners, walking barefoot in the sand; the tanks, planes, all the Soviet equipment charred and grounded. All the strategists in the world, and the French more than all the others, commented on the military genius of the Israeli leaders, and decided to include these battles in the curricula of their military schools. The minuscule State is suddenly swollen with all its conquests. Mourning in the Arab world, triumph in the West, among all the Jews. But in the Third World also there is respect for their cleverness, their strength, their superiority.

Israel as Will and
as Representation

When force has this sort of spectacular quality, there are always poets and crowds who will find aspects of justice in it, Stendhal notes in speaking of the Napoleonic campaigns, in which he himself took part, and for which he did not conceal his admiration. We know—and de Gaulle has been credited with prescience on this subject—that this 1967 victory changed the face of the world. In fact it is from this Arab humiliation that the idea took shape after the Yom Kippur War in 1973: the idea of proletarian nations using oil as weapon.

But even after the Eichmann trial and the reawakening of the memory of genocide, this victory continued to change the behavior of Jews and their relationship to Israel. It is quite strange, in fact, to note that it was a show of strength, an assertion by military victory, that made a number of Jews discover the intensity of Judaism, the permanence of its "roots," the solidity of their connections with Jewish tradition.

The recapture of Jerusalem, with all its Biblical connotations, all the poetic and traditional overtones of the very name of the Holy City, the rediscovered possibility of praying at the Wailing Wall—all that made people feel a need to reassert themselves as Jewish.

And surely this return to Judaism was also helped along by the disappointment aroused by the transformations of Stalinism and even of Communism. All the more so

since, for the very people who did not give up their
Socialist hopes, the decision was made—just as it was for
the feminists—not to expect a solution for the Jewish problem from the revolution, and certainly not to wait for the
revolution to find a solution. Networks of support and solidarity multiplied. Tourism by activists, the faithful, and
the curious was never more intense. The prestige of everything Jewish was unequalled. Some great European intellectuals were tempted by Israeli nationality. Today they are
pro-Palestinian—and often unhappy at having to be so.

Mutations   The most secular Jews, the least traditional, the ones most
ignorant of their culture, the most "de-judaified," as
Raymond Aron said, began to feel a renewal of interest and
sometimes of passion for Jewish matters. As to the pro-Arab
Jews, they told themselves sotto voce that Israel had finally
cleansed the Jewish people of all accusations of cowardliness, inaptitude for combat, flight when faced with peril.
They were now in a situation to benefit from the consequences of a cause—Zionism—that they claimed to disown.

To return to the immense majority, it is a strange thing
that it was thanks to a victory that protected the people
from persecution and genocide that the Jews began to turn
their attention once again to the recent past, to the
Holocaust, the camps, and the attitude of various nations,
especially the French. Contrary to what is being written

*Israel as Will and
as Representation*

today, the Jews of France did not rediscover their ancient fears when Israel was weak and isolated, but rather after Israel had become a victor. It is as if, once they were certain of the solidity of the refuge-State, confident in its strength and its future, alerted to how the faith of their ancestors could raise mountains, these Jews allowed themselves to acknowledge the truth about the anti-Semitism surrounding them, and even felt that in order to avenge their past they had to unearth it again and remind a world that suddenly admired Israel what it had done to the Jews before. By making the memory of the Shoah sacred, they thus participated a little in the Israeli victories. Jewish sadness had to be present for them for Israeli happiness to be complete—and justified. Now that they were sure of being able to defend themselves, they swore they would never again put themselves in the situation of being persecuted. The people soon became unjust and vindictive.

The observation I feel obliged to offer here comes in the case of the same Jews who, when they were forming their opinions on the future of the Near East, and on the politics of France before 1967, expressed a detached pessimism on the behavior of the Israelis, and did not admit that the fate of the Jews of the world could be closely tied with the fortunes and misfortunes of Israel. Now these Jews, having drawn closer to the victorious State after 1967, would have worried a thousand times more about the fate of the Jewish communities throughout the world if

Israel's isolation were to be increased. In other words, it was the Israeli victory that intensified the ties of the new Jerusalem with the Jews of the diaspora, and that revived Judaism in places that had been de-judaified, or as we try not to say today, "assimilated."

A Perpetual War?

Every Israeli was now revealed to be invaluable as a soldier, not as a witness; as a fighter, not as a messenger. The advent of Israel became a rupture. This advent was substituted for the coming of the Messiah. It is not recognized as such since all the Jews of the world did not flock to it. But it became a shield as much against secular hostility as against surrounding aggression. It made the ancient hope less keen, and the wait less necessary. If it prevented Jews from settling elsewhere, it was less with the thought of keeping themselves free for a universal or heavenly Jerusalem, than of defending this earthly Jerusalem, reconquered and threatened. People no longer lived in the hope and faith of the conquered, but in the fear and trembling of conquerors. From the moment when there was no more "next year in Jerusalem," since it's today in Jerusalem, the virtue of hope became less important than the other traditional virtues. The Jews are under construction, at war, in a state of emergency, in active mobilization. All the more so since, as Ben-Gurion said, they "cannot allow themselves to lose a war."

Israel as Will and
as Representation

But can they give themselves permission to wage any war at all, even a defensive one? And for how long? "Given to Israel, the land still remains the property of God, and the people can consider themselves at home only if they welcome it permanently as a gift. *The country is mine; in my abode, you are exiles and guests*." Though the gift is definite, the actual possession of it is conditional: In the most severe words, the Book of Deuteronomy prophesies that the people of Israel will be driven from its land if it is unfaithful to the Covenant. And that is where we find the cruel caprice of a god who bestows on His people a land whose defense implies fidelity to the Covenant, of course, but also a betrayal of Election and of the Ten Commandments.

V.
Life and Death

Know now that God hath overthrown me,
and hath compassed me with his net.

Job 19:6.

"A life is worth nothing, but nothing is worth a life": The wisdom of Ecclesiastes, reinterpreted by Malraux, is not even literally true to Jewish tradition. To say that a life is worth nothing is to start weighing the value of life whereas, obviously, as texts and actions prove, it is life itself that is value. One does not wonder about the value of value. Or if one does, suicide or nihilism is the result. Life should thus serve as a criterion, and contradiction would take place only when suffering becomes unbearable. It is only in Alfred de Vigny that Moses, weary of being powerful and alone, wants to sleep the sleep of the earth. Job suffers from all his calamities, but does he want to die? Perhaps what we call Messianism is the hope for hope, hope that is life, hope that the suffering will stop, life that contains Evil but also its opposite. Eternity of the Breath-of-Life.

On this account, Messianism rejects the coming of the Messiah. Messianism is all expectation, all hope. Wasn't recognizing the Messiah in Christ somehow a way of suppressing hope and life, as well as anticipation? Christianity, by gratifying expectations, impoverished one of its theological virtues: hope. Christianity was led to desacralize the present, to declare that the kingdom was not of this world, and to make people live in guilty exile on this earth while awaiting eternal life. But perhaps that is the cost some authors were willing to concede when they spoke of pagan survivals in both Judaism and Islam, and thus they can assert an opposition between Christianity and life. When Christ said, "I am the resurrection and eternal life," even though he came among humans to say it, he did not come to them *only* to say this. Suffering here will find its justification only in the promise, withdrawn each time, of a recompense elsewhere. For the Jews, however, everything must happen in this world.

I propose to show how this leads to a unique relationship between the Jew and death. The organization of survival is, in threatened species as well as in persecuted minorities, the subject of ancient and precise observations. It is an organization that implies semi-secrecy, coordinated activities, networks of support, an unfailing solidarity, unchangeable structures. These are the characteristics of all more or less secret societies, all the *Freemasonic* organizations and guilds that know everywhere in the world how to seek each other out, find each other, make sure they are recognized, aided, sheltered, protected. The society as a whole is the object of such heavy and constant menaces that each of its members becomes very precious. Everyone watches out for the life of everyone else, and the death of any one of them is felt as the harbinger of decay, if not of annihilation.

It is probably this threatening dimension that explains in part the individual Jew, who, surrounded by Gentiles, has a much more subjective and particular awareness of death than his neighbors. It is interesting to note that suicide entered Jewish society at a time when it was unknown (and would remain so for a long time) in African, Arab, Near-Eastern, and even Western societies. Suicide, in effect, implies an overestimation of individual life. One asks oneself if it can be endured or not only because one has a personal way of experiencing it. One no longer shares with the tribe the faculty of responding impersonally to the rhythms and alternations of the world. Or rather, more precisely, one shares with the tribe only a respect for life, in a struggle against mortality. That is the opposite of integration with the world and of submission of culture to nature. The world is not seen as a representation but as a will. Of course, it will be the will of God to watch over His people so that it can express His truth through their testimony. But this is to be expressed by a love of life, a vigilant, jealous, fearful, and superstitious attachment to all that supports, favors, and exalts life.

The Pure Present   Many centuries have shaped this people in a veritable fear of death. Surely the form of worship maintained in all

the Jewish Prison
Jean Daniel

ancient societies, and in biblical communities, with a
patriarch in contact with the gods, and heeding the advice
of these Ancients who, linked to both heaven and earth,
caused the nobility of death to be accepted, no doubt those
rites contributed to a fear of premature death, death strik
ing before the wisdom and knowledge of old age. The fact
remains that, even in the heart of the most Mediterranean
society, the most familial structure, the Jews had a carnal,
religious devotion to their children. A child that is born is
not just a possible inheritor and, if he is male, the bearer
of the father's name: He is the proof that the species will
last, that the message is being transmitted, that identity is
being asserted and continued, that testimony will be given,
that the chosen people will be multitudinous enough, when
the day comes, to show that, worthy of its Election, it can
welcome the Messiah.

All this must give rise to men of cunning rather than
men of risk, of enjoyment rather than sacrifice, of hope
rather than combat. For Louis Massignon, the great
Islamist and Catholic mystic, "Islam represents faith, the
Jews, hope, Christianity, charity." There we recognize the
three theological virtues. Thinkers like Levinas do not
accept this distinction. Hope meant returning to Zion; it
was the hope that the phrase "next year in Jerusalem"
summarized. But it had to be accompanied by charity
(recognition of the Other) and by faith in the universal.

Pindar's famous exhortation—"Oh my soul, do not seek the absolute but exhaust the field of the possible"—could also easily be biblically inspired. In all the Mediterranean societies where they have taken root, Jewish communities have obviously shared all the taboos and prejudices, all the culinary, sexual, and domestic customs. But death, and the dead, have never been the object of the same kind of worship or the same ceremonies. The sense of the present, receptiveness to happiness, respect for the father, sexual taboos, culinary nostalgia: All those things can be found in the Moroccan Berbers, the Andalusians, Sicilians, Maltese, and all the Mediterranean peoples. But in these people one also finds a submission to death, or a way of integrating its sudden eruption into daily life, which is lacking in the Jewish people. Death is always a scandal for the Jews, as if life were always a blessing.

In a book that is often quite moving, *Tolède ou le Secret du Greco* (Toledo or the secret of El Greco), Maurice Barrès, the master of our modern French Romantics, interpreted the *Guide of the Wanderers* by the Andalusian Maimonides as a manual of treachery supposed to obtain for the chosen people the thousand and one formulae to interpret, to their own advantage, the laws of the countries where dispersion forced them to live. Barrès, who pushed deep-rooted racism to such a point that he deplored having to discern, among the most beautiful Spanish women,

traces revealing a Jewish or Moorish ancestry, unhappy all
the more so at having to wonder if after all it wasn't this
very ancestry that gave the Spanish woman her insolent
beauty—Barrès, then, had enough keenness and percep-
tion to feel that there was something to be discovered in
the relationships between the Jews and death. He discovered this in Spain, a civilization in which we know the
position death holds. And he did so on the subject of a
sense of honor. Less full of hatred and less fanatical than
his disciple Charles Maurras would be, and less philosophical, perhaps, than the latter, Barrès did not think this
Spanish Jewish community was cowardly. He wondered
whether there wasn't a communal and religious sense of
honor that commanded the faithful never to risk, individually, in a duel for instance, a life that one owed to God.

Excessive Gift I do not know if the latest word in sociology entails excluding the concept of a collective soul, or a collective unconscious. I think the more commonly used term is collective
imagination. In any case, if there is a precious notion for
what occupies us here, it is the one Freud employs at the end
of his life in *Moses and Monotheism* (his most-discussed book
because of certain historical errors that pedants have pointed out with the smugness much in favor at certain universities). All this—which is just my ill humor—is in aid of
saying that, throughout these "approximations," I am only

Life and Death

attempting an interpretation, nourished by various readings and experiences, precisely of this collective soul.

The wish to gather together, to remain among one's own people, to protect each other, watch over each other, cherish each other, arm each other—all led to an immense and fundamental rejection of death, as we have seen. But, to return to Barrès, one could say that we can judge the degree of integration of Jews into societies where they chose to live by observing their faculty of dying. This is true not because this faculty is the sign of a kind of belonging, but because, for a traditional Jew, haunted by the age-old subconscious of his tradition, and drawing from it the roots of his reflexes, to give his life for something other than Judaism is the supreme sign of a salutary sharing.

On this account, one can say, for instance, that the German Jews and the Alsatian Jews, during the First World War, gave evidence of settling in their respective homelands. We know, moreover, how many German Jews were German. I have already cited the strange case of a German, Nahum Goldman—a personality who played a large role in obtaining reparations after the war, reparations that Germany would pay in order to participate in the construction of the State of Israel—who dared to assert that nothing was more like German genius than Jewish genius, that either could—in his opinion!—be confused with the other. This was by no means the sign of his Jewish lucidity, but of his German patriotism.

the Jewish Prison
Jean Daniel

Often I wonder—in fact, it's mostly because I am asked—what there is that is "Jewish" about me. I wind up by thinking that perhaps it's this attitude towards death. I have explained this elsewhere, but, it seems to me, with imprecision and hence misunderstanding. I mean that what I respect most in this Jewish specificity, and thus what I would most like to recognize in myself, is this relationship to death, which entrains a particular relationship to suffering and to Evil. It is this relationship that is made clear when, finally, the walls of the Jewish prison disappear, and when otherness is no longer singularity, ordeal, or conflict, but rather an invitation to the gift.

This famous phrase is attributed to Madame du Deffand: "The unfortunate thing is to be born, and yet we can say of this misfortune that the remedy is worse than the illness." Let us note in passing that Cioran did not say it better. Marie du Deffand, a marquise, whose salon welcomed all the Encyclopédistes, makes clear she prefers an impossible life to no life at all. Let us adapt the same maxim for the use of some Jews: "The unfortunate thing is to be born Jewish, and yet we can say of this misfortune that the cure (here: no longer being Jewish) is worse than the disease." That is what Heinrich Heine ended up thinking. That is what, without confessing it, sometimes without even admitting it to themselves, a number of believing and unbelieving Jews have thought. For we have understood that since the Shoah, no moving away, even in misfortune, is conceivable to them. For Spinoza, it was not a question of no longer being Jewish but, by emancipation and assimilation, of making religion a private matter. That meant exposing oneself to the risk of the disappearance of the Jews as a people. And that is what was most shocking in the solitary philosopher from Amsterdam. "Choose political Zionism, then," he replied. But could he have done so after the Shoah and after the State of Israel? Before these injunctions and these impasses I would like, for my part, to maintain unchanged the tension between the two poles of united exteriority and critical belonging. I do not see the necessity, here or elsewhere, of emerging from a questioning that I have made my philosophy and that is, in every point, hostile to theological thought.

Conclusion

Moreover the Lord answered Job,
and said,
Shall he that contendeth with the Almighty
instruct *him*?

Job 40:1-2.

The Jews
Believe in
Their Myths

I write these lines at a time when twilight over fields of desolation is more a harbinger of end-of-the-world tempests than of the dawns of great beginnings. One can hear the voices of martyred children mixed with the cries of rebels coming from the sepulchral depths, voices and cries shouting dismayed questions at heaven. Still burning, covered with embers, the ashes of the victims of Auschwitz and Birkenau, of Hiroshima and the Gulag, and streaming out to join them the victims of Cambodia and Rwanda, and this was our twentieth century. And now, from this Promised Land, three times holy and celebrated with so much insistence by the Creator to emphasize the incomparable virtues of the offering made to His creation, the dawn of the twenty-first century is breaking, baptized by the blood and tears of Palestinian and Israeli orphans.

I also write these final pages, however, during a journey to Greece in the Cyclades, blessed by the gods. Never throughout a journey that has already been long, either in Tipasa, in Sidi Bu Said, in Porto Ercole, in Bonifacio, or in

the Jewish Prison
Jean Daniel

Lipari, have I seen the Mediterranean so dazzling with its benevolent light. Beauty is never so intense, and it is never so much itself, as when the need we have for it becomes obvious and profound. Indifferent to the suffering populations that line its shores, this sovereign sea procures for people the eternal convalescence that survives the body's decay. Mythological shades hover here. That of Achilles, who emerges from adolescence only to choose the glory of a heroic and premature death. That of Ulysses, who accumulates exploits only to end his days at home returning to Penelope's side, after having refused to be the equal of a god. Intensity or Duration. To be a hero or a wise man. That is the alternative that, since Antiquity, Mediterraneans have offered the world. But Athens is not Jerusalem. And Joshua, like Mohammed later on, also a warlord, refuses to choose. He means to unite in himself alone the flame and the light. Which is to say, the Absolute.

Finally, I am writing in days when Palestinian mothers wander haggard in the ruins of their devastated houses, and when the finest sons of Israel begin to wonder about the future of their young State, and even about the meaning of their combat. Israel was until recently, like the United States, and moreover partly thanks to the U.S., the strongest. But since even possession of nuclear weapons cannot discourage any kamikaze, or shelter any might, we no longer know where the strength is located now.

Conclusion

As a passionate witness to the evolution of affairs, I think I can assert that none of them was compelled by unalterable destiny. The misfortune of them all was the liberty of each. On the other hand, I have watched how and at what point some form of theological thought, after being banished by the pioneers of Israel and the Palestinian laypeople, fed the strategies of extremists and conquerors. And I recall that the unbelievers have never truly called into question the biblical, hence "revealed," origin of their State.

How could beings so shaped by culture, so devoutly respectful of knowledge, so careful to communicate a taste for knowledge to their children, so determined to place Creativity and Mind above the delights of money and the temptations of power, yes, how can such beings deny themselves the simple demands of reason and the obvious facts of truth? They know, they cannot act as if they didn't know, that you cannot fashion an absolute by metaphors, apologias, or invocations. Why do they act as if there were no flood before Noah's, as if there were no Tables of the Law before those of Moses, as if there was no Mesopotamia before the birth of Israel? "Did the Greeks believe in their myths?" wonders the historian Paul Veyne. Answer: No, of course not. But the Jews? Yes! Unlike the supernatural elements in the *Iliad* and the *Odyssey*, those in the Hebrew Bible are intimately associated with the history of a people. For separation of the legendary from the historical is impossible if both are dictated by Revelation.

The Israelis, and especially their Jewish and Christian friends, should understand that it is not in their interest to refer to the Revelation, the Covenant, or the Book, except as wonderfully founding mythologies. For we have seen, finally, that if we were to sacralize the idea of Election as an injunction to be the best, it is not possible to ignore the verses in Deuteronomy that recall that the land given to Israel belongs to others. And God insists: "And it shall be, when the Lord thy God shall have brought thee into the land which he sware unto thy fathers, to Abraham, to Isaac, and to Jacob, to give thee great and goodly cities, which thou buildedst not, And houses full of all good *things*, which thou filledst not, and wells digged, which thou diggedst not, vineyards and olive trees, which thou plantedst not" (Deut. 6:10-11). In other words, if one wants to use providential logic as evidence, God reminds us that Israel must deserve a right of ownership that it does not possess. By its behavior, Israel must make people forget that it is a foreigner in a foreign land. We could say that in 1948 the peoples of the world decided that, because of its sufferings and its allies, Israel deserved to re-establish itself on a land that for a long time had not been its own.

Return and Function of Anti-Semitism

Before the crushing contradictions of this state of affairs, and as if to escape from it, an old Jewish distress has seized the diaspora. It arouses, in the United States and France

Conclusion

especially, the notion of the return of eternal anti-Semitism in unexpected forms. Some intellectuals, whose solitary courage I respect, have let themselves go as far as maintaining that a *pro-Palestinian anti-racism* might transform into anti-Semitism, in accusing the Jews of having become executioners as cruel as those whose victims they had been. Emotions, even more legitimate and justified confronting the multiplication of anti-Semitic acts, from graffiti to insults, brutality in schools, arson in synagogues, are all the keener when public opinion seems indifferent.

The fact remains that the theoreticians of this revival of Evil neglect in general to remember the extraordinary popularity of Israel at the time of its birth, then during its epic and its victories, and, finally, after the peace treaty with Egypt and the Oslo agreements. Nowhere did we find in those days any trace of *pro-Palestinian racism* against the Jews. Then, the same analysts decided to overinterpret the clearly anti-Semitic—obvious, and alarming—drift of the feelings of solidarity with the Palestinians—feelings that at the outset were aroused by constant televised pounding of information about Israeli repression of rebellious youth in the outlying districts, for the most part abandoned sons of poor Arab immigrants. Finally, what the best minds have not resigned themselves to accepting, is that the compassionate regard for the Jews has radically changed. For the profit, benefit, and glory of their respective nations, Jews have rediscovered their

the Jewish Prison
Jean Daniel

"ancient splendor" in Jerusalem, in New York, and in Paris. They are represented in all the corridors of authority and creativity. They arouse in other communities an admiration that is soon transformed into envy. Because of their unique ordeals during the Shoah, they have tended to monopolize interest and pity.

Given this new way of looking at them, how can we think that the Jews remain basically the same? And are still close to finding themselves once again in the role of victims? And that this role has prevented them from being clear about the reasons that might have motivated an alarmed anxiety in response to the behavior of certain Israeli governments that fell into an exploitation of theology? As to the indifference of public opinion, it has often manifested in those who got the impression that the same Jews who needed them before could now make it on their own. This is neither an excuse, nor even an extenuating circumstance. But it is an explanation that one has the right to offer to keep from having to explain—for fear of seeming to "understand" it—a phenomenon that can resemble the Shoah.

Actually, in certain cases, or really in many cases, the obsessive, organized, and aggressive fear of anti-Semitism as well as denunciation of it have had, at root, the intention to ward it off. Even for those who had no interest in exploiting it and whose anguish was fed by the memory of tragedy,

Conclusion

this fear has had a dangerously negative effect. It has allowed people to avoid the questions that arose about whether or not one should fall into line with the policies of Israel. Théo Klein went so far as to say—with the boldness that is characteristic of him and the authority he draws from the fact of also being Israeli—that there was a certain *jubilatory comfort* for a new generation to rediscover the victim State and its justification. For the ex-victim, there was no longer a risk of being treated as a "new executioner," since he was rediscovering the condition of being a victim.

The Dilemma of Leo Strauss

As I was finishing this essay, and although in order to write it I imposed on myself the rule of not getting distracted by the profusion and intimidating monthly literary overproduction about the Jews, I discovered Leo Strauss's essay "Why We Remain Jews".[6] I understood immediately that one could not, that I could not, ignore the German philosopher's answers to questions that are our own, and my own, especially today.

Leo Strauss is a singular philosopher. Hannah Arendt, Karl Jaspers, Franz Rosenzweig all had a fascinated esteem for him, sometimes despite themselves. He passed through all the stages of Jewish mediation as just so many moments in human thought. But what has caused him to emerge conspicuously in recent days and in an unfortunate way is the fact that the American neo-conservatives,

---

[6] "Why We Remain Jews," *Jewish Philosophy and the Crisis of Modernity*, translated by Kenneth Hart Green (Albany: SUNY Press, 1997).

right-wing ideologues, thought they could claim to be his followers. After all, anti-Semites claimed to be followers of Nietzsche, and even sometimes of Bergson.

Before he was a professor at Chicago, Leo Strauss grew up in Germany in a family of orthodox Jews from which he freed himself first by a passionate involvement with Spinoza, and then by what amounted to a conversion to an *atheist Zionism.* He preferred this solution to an assimilation that in Germany did not settle the Jewish problem. Strauss became an activist involved in the cause of political Zionism: another way of remaining faithful to Spinoza's criticism of the religion.

First of all, Leo Strauss continued to think of Zionism as aiming above all to restore honor to the Jewish people "and to cleanse it from its age-old degeneration" by the creation of an independent, national State. This conversion of Leo Strauss to Zionism would distance him even more radically from Jewish religion. In his opinion, the fate of the Jews in effect depends on the action of people in their new State, and not on the divine intervention that they might passively expect. Political Zionism takes a severe view of any Messianic anticipation.

Secondly, there must be a State that gathers together a people, for "the uprooted, assimilated Jew has nothing with which to confront hatred and scorn except his naked ego." But this Zionism would have to be cultural, "because it would be nothing but an empty shell without a Jewish

Conclusion

culture plunging its roots into Jewish heritage." Here we find *historicist voluntarism*, that is to say the wish not to be separated from historic fidelity to the past of the Jewish people, but still without evoking any kind of transcendence.

Finally, and thirdly, Leo Strauss asserts, while still claiming to remain an atheist himself, that, without belief in a Revelation, it is not possible to desire to remain Jewish.

But the great, single idea is precisely, in Leo Strauss's opinion as well as that of so many others, to remain Jewish—in order to remain Jewish. There is no reason to be so, except that one has been so. One does not leave one's camp; one does not flee one's roots; one does not desert one's people; one does not escape one's fate; one does not fail one's honor. One must raise one's head and keep it high, and Jewish genius allows this. Imposing, fierce consistency! These are pleas in the form of self-sufficient, tautological, peremptory postulates.

I am because I am. This irrevocable decision is shouted out by prisoners who obviously fear being tempted to leave the prison, and who order the others to remain within it. Why this rage to persevere in one's existence if one doesn't have somewhere the secret and private impression that it can't be done? There is nothing more edifying than this obligation Leo Strauss felt to locate a definite meaning (especially in the Bible) in what had never had meaning for him before.

How could I not respect those who want to "remain Jewish"? Without saying so, my ancestors wanted to do so for generations, I suppose. They did so as quietly as possible, in the privacy of their own family. God walked home with my father. He believed He was there when he went to sleep. I do not have the feeling that I am being unfaithful to him when I discover that I myself am more anxious to know where my fate is leading me than I am to escape it; I am more anxious to take a census of my different roots than to be faithful to any one of them; more anxious at the end of each day to verify that my honor is indeed where my conscience has set it rather than make sure it's not been slighted.

Nor do I have the feeling of infidelity when I reflect that if one truly wishes to be a Jew—in conformity with the Election—one must above all seek in sacred history, in the Book, in the revelation, for what is compatible with the Universal.

But it is true that, after witnessing the tragedies of the Near East in 2003, I came to the conclusion that the Jews should retain from their Election only the command to be the best, and from the Covenant only the obligation to make Israel a beacon for other nations. If that is deemed impossible, then everyone is Jewish and no one is. The prison then remains cruel, glorious, absurd, eternal. Like the human condition? Yes, indeed. But it is not humanity's business to choose voluntary servitude.

Simone Weil,
or, The Greek
and The Jew

What I passionately desire is not to be approved of but to be understood. I emphasized from the beginning my lacunae and inadequacies. Even if they are less unfathomable than they were before writing this book, they remain enormous. However, I took the decision, surely a rash one, not to think of them as handicaps requiring silence. In one sense, quite the opposite is true. For I am less concerned with what God said than I am with the reasons for which He was made to say what He said. The different and successive versions of the Pentateuch arouse exegeses beyond my competence but not beyond my observation.

As far as I know, it is not disputed that the Jewish people defines itself, to begin with, by the fact that it benefits from Election and the Covenant. The only objection made to this definition, which is too simple for the Talmudists as well as for unbelievers, is that people want to be defined as Jews without thinking that they belong to the chosen people or that they are linked to a god by a Covenant. An absurd argument. A religion can be entirely secularized. The Christians prove that to us every day. But also: Judaism has nothing, it is sometimes said, to do with faith. In a delightful story told by Théo Klein, a young student comes, alarmed, to consult his rabbi. He says to him, "Rabbi, it's terrible, I think I have lost faith." And the angry rabbi dismisses the student, telling him not to mix everything up and to study the Bible well without thinking about "anything at all." We can make allowances for the joke. But there is a curious elation in such an act of separating God from His people, and the Bible from its author. What remains of the Jew when he believes neither in Election, nor in the Covenant, nor in God? Spinoza replied: "Nothing." Nothing, except common memories of persecution, the observance of family feasts and celebrations, the same way of honoring one's parents and one's dead. A sense of humor, finally, but one so linked to despair that, for at least five years, the conquerors, dazzled by the Yom Kippur War, were deprived of it.

In any case, and once again, the important thing is not so much to know what believing Jews say themselves about their belief, but why unbelievers behave as if they do believe, especially after the Shoah and the return to Zion. The latter live riveted to the universe built by the former. Where the unbeliever accepts a yoke, the believer experiences a blessing.

People will say that any meditation on one of the great religions and one of the great ethical systems leads one to stress the limits of a human being. And to overestimate, by doing so, the capacities of man to follow religious and moral precepts. In fact we see clearly that any summons to follow the paths of holiness and any command to travel them to the end comes down to deliberately, and even cunningly, demanding the impossible. It is true that in

Conclusion

Islam it is a question of a "marveling submission." To be dazzled, the seclusion must be no less complete. After reading Simone Weil's *The Need for Roots*, I wind up thinking that its author is saying that God put all humans in the same prison and that, simply, Israel went in first, without recognizing that Christ could have broken its bars. Ought I say here that I believe none of this? Christians had the immense merit of inventing for themselves an incarnate god to share the suffering of men, but they found someone even more unbearable: One who teaches them that you must offer your left cheek after the right has been slapped, must answer violence with love. That is not exactly what Saint Bernard would later preach to the Knights Templar.

Impossible and Indispensable Holiness

In any case, for my part, thinking only of the Jews, I have tried to show or, to be more modest, to recall that the greatest Jewish thinkers, from Martin Buber to Emmanuel Levinas, and including Franz Rosenzweig and Gershom Sholem, put all their energy into redefining the terms "Election" and "Covenant," so that the Jewish people can no longer claim the exclusivity of either. Once again, to summarize this idea in simpler words, according to them, God conceived of a calling for the Jews that is specific only in excellence, never in character or superiority. God founded an aristocracy, that is to say a caste of the best, whose behavior should be a contagious exemplarity, closed to no one. Each person can thus choose to become a saint, that is to say, Jewish. All the other interpretations then become, according to the thinkers I cited above, veritable heresies. Then why have people asserted the opposite for so long and so often, and why did they so commit themselves? It is not even certain that the idea of a chosen people, for which, thanks to the Covenant, a privileged fate and a status of superiority were preserved, where rights won out over duties, did not in fact originate in an anti-Semitic tradition or, more precisely, one fundamentally hostile to Judaism since the first century. Christians, especially those adhering to the councils and the Fathers of the Church, would not be unfamiliar with this interpretation.

In this case, I have permitted myself, throughout these pages, to put an equals sign between the caste of the best and that of the just, and between the class of aristocrats and that of the saints. If the Jews have no other calling than to be priests and witnesses, then one can say that Judaism is entirely an exhortation to holiness. And that really, in my opinion, was the case for all religions before Churches became organized and took charge of the message. In other words, there can be a Jewish people according to the history of a community that has striven to be special and continuous. But, for God, in humanity, and obedient to the divine logic with which He is concerned, the chosen people stop being Jewish, and the Jewish people stop being chosen, as soon as it devotes itself to something other than testimony and priesthood.

Now, for the unbelievers. Those who are attached only to the history of mankind and to the historicity of texts; those for whom Revelation has no meaning, inasmuch as God, having no existence, has nothing to reveal; those who say they scrupulously observe the rites out of respect for their forebears or out of solidarity with the persecuted, or out of a wish not to be renegades or victims of self-hatred: All of them behave like religious people who, not feeling that they are the ones summoned to holiness, chose to make their emotional nest and find their spiritual blossoming in family or in a community that persecution periodically strengthens.

In a certain sense, one could say that believers have gratefully accepted incarceration in this monastery-prison from which they could not escape without abjuring their vow of fidelity and belonging. Unbelievers, on the other hand, chose voluntarily, deliberately, and continuously to live in a prison where holiness was no longer being practiced, and whose bars they built themselves, but where they do not rule out the possibility of a hidden god punishing them for wanting to leave. In the end, to leave prison is to leave oneself. The unbelievers feel even more "chosen" than the others. But they do not know it.

the Jewish Prison
Jean Daniel

War and
Peace

All these reflections were confirmed in my eyes by the realization of the promise in a foreign Holy Land, yesterday Canaan, today Palestine. Concerning Israel, the reader who wants to refer to my collected writings over almost fifty years will discover feelings in which admiration and empathy, especially in the beginning, are vigorously manifest. I even wrote about my debt to the Israelis, and I went so far as to say that the disappearance of the Jewish State as the Socialist pioneers dreamed of it would make me in part an orphan. It was, and it remains, a fine dream, a human dream, one it is not necessary to Judaify, or attach to it a god liberal with promises.

That was after the 1967 victory, at a time when General Dayan told me that Palestinian children were as dear to him as his own. Those are moving phrases, over which I linger on account of the evolution of my feelings, not, of course, about the State of Israel in the principle of its existence, which is dear to me, but about Israeli governments. For I thought that the Jewish pioneers often thought of the Palestinians with as little respect as God had when He dispossessed the Canaanites from their land. I thought one ought to do much better than this capricious, colonizing god, whose seigniorial generosity manifested itself at the expense of a people that was nonetheless also summoned to holiness to join the chosen people.

In the 1980's, the famous American journalist Flora Lewis invited me to meet a man at the Ritz who she said

was very powerful, since he was the president of the World
Jewish Congress and a multimillionaire. Executive, I think,
of a famous brand of whiskey. I can still picture this scene.
In his slovenly drunkenness, the multimillionaire remained
flamboyant. He was not a priest, not a witness, not a saint,
not a just man. An arrogant skeleton supporting sagging
muscles. When my turn to be presented to him came, I was
treated to a conceited lecture he uttered without looking at
me. He announced that I had the honor of being present at
a celebration, his own, to celebrate a treaty of solidarity he
had extracted from the archbishop of New York, Cardinal
Spellman, I think. It was only my silence that made him
suddenly take an interest in me. He asked me why I seemed
so unmoved by such a success. I replied that it seemed to
me more important today to conclude a treaty with the
Arabs, and especially with the Palestinians, rather than
with Christians who were ready to do anything to remove
the guilt of their indirect and distant participation in the
Shoah. Flora Lewis took me away so as to avoid, she told me
later, the aggressively sarcastic remarks which the zealous
sycophants of this businessman would make.

An anecdote. A true friend, whom I hadn't seen in a
long time, visited me a few weeks later to invite me to take
part in a Committee to Defend and Celebrate Jerusalem
along with a Nobel Prize-winner, a bishop, a minister, and
several bankers. So I asked which of them was an Arab. He
said to me, with perfect sincerity, "You know, we hadn't

thought of including a Muslim, an Arab, or a Palestinian in this committee." Since he was a friend, I told him how that omission alarmed me, whether it was owing to irresponsible indifference, or the most distressing scorn. All this is to say that the obsession of the Jews in the diaspora has been to maintain solidarity with the rediscovered Holy Land and with the defenders of the Holy City, but it has not been to be faithful to the Election or to the Covenant, as they have been defined by my great Jewish thinkers.

*Return to
Jerusalem*

At this moment in my narrative, I must return to Jerusalem, if only, this time, in thought. How did this city come about? Was it truly promised? To whom does it belong? How many times does its name figure in the Hebrew Bible, in the Gospels, or in the Koran? I won't discuss that here, although my religion, it should be said, is constructed around a small number of facts. For if I take an interest in these questions, it is not in order to answer them, but to emphasize that they exist, that people have asked them, that the heirs of Abraham, of Moses, of Jesus, and of Mohammed have wanted to ask them.

Already, this mere fact has always seemed enormous to me and, to tell the truth, less and less bearable. As I was strolling with the Dominican whom I mentioned in the first lines of this essay, we passed in front of the Armenian

Conclusion

cathedral of Jerusalem, and I heard my guide recall, with troubled gentleness, that Pope John Paul II, quite recently, had been unable to enter it because the Armenian Apostolic Church denied the authority of the Vatican. Everyone knows what is going on between the different Christian sects, the representatives of the different Muslim schisms, and all the clans of religious Jews. After all, that might not have had any importance, and we could have talked about this city as we speak of Amsterdam, when Rembrandt was painting his masterpieces in the Jewish quarter and where people from all the countries of Europe went to admire such harmony in the coexistence of three religions that there was no reason to envy that of medieval Andalusia.

We have done the same with Jerusalem. We should have done so. It is unendurable that we cannot speak of Jerusalem as we spoke of Cordoba or Amsterdam. If there is a city where the inspiration of men and divine mercy could have united to make just one single light of hope gleam, to make reign over the city peace between citizens of good will, to transform swords into ploughshares and hatred into brotherhood, that should have been, that could only have taken place, in this place of Election and sanctification, where all the proofs of the Covenant are in principle joined together. How can we accept the fact that Jerusalem has not been the cathedral where the poor, the persecuted, and the sinners could come to take refuge

the Jewish Prison
Jean Daniel

thanks to a right to asylum that no one could revoke, and where no army, no weapon, could penetrate? The fact that people can wage war in Jerusalem has seemed to me, ever since I learned the history of the Frankish kingdom and of the Crusades, like a desecration, a paganization of a place that has miraculously remained magical and that reveals all the wounds—never healed—of the world.

But when, in 1967, the city was reunified, then we began to believe, or those close to it did, in a mission given again by God to the chosen people to make peace, tolerance, and—who knows?—even love, be respected. In short, to make Canaan be forgotten. Today, this illusion seems like an unfathomable absurdity. In any case, if I had wanted any additional proof of the sadistic caprice with which God treated His people (or His peoples), or of the masochism with which these same peoples had invented for themselves this three-times-holy city, it is obvious that Jerusalem has supplied it for me.

Now we are in the domain of the inexcusable, the irretrievable, and the unthinkable. The inventors of a unique God and His demand for unbounded love, the monotheists who imagined the meaning of History and who broke with the tragic have transformed the City of Light, the symbolic capital, into a simple Greek city where the battles of the blind sons of Atreus take place in the darkness. You have to be an unfeeling soul indeed to resist this

Conclusion

insult offered to reason and compassion. In cases like this, they say, you simply have to have faith. But, if you don't have faith, how can you get it at such a price? It is like the paradox of the minor prophets of the Babylonian era: "To love God, you have to know Him, and to know Him, you have to love Him." The fact remains that, when I learn that Palestinian fanatics are shooting at Jews at prayer, and that an Israeli extremist is beating Palestinians prostrate before the tomb of Abraham, then I tell myself that the prison of the Jews has become the prison of everyone.

The most curious thing, in this story, is that, every time I tell it, there is always someone, generally a believer, who abandons the domain of faith and takes refuge in "fatalist" explanations. To my question, "How is belief possible?", he'll reply, That's how people are. But it is precisely not simply a story of human nature! And in any case, this story isn't unfolding just anywhere! In Jerusalem, since time without memory men have aspired to a surpassing, a transcendence of self; they have imagined a higher order. That is what it is to be human. And, if he has decided, against all vanities, to practice what they call his *profession*, then he must look every day, every instant, for justice and charity, without wondering in whom a capricious god chooses to incarnate to defend them. For if one has to look at things from God's point of view, I really don't see why, suddenly, every time I ask myself the questions that Job or

the Jewish Prison
Jean Daniel

Pascal posed, it's Zeus or Sophocles who answers me. I am willing to die for whatever universal quality the Jews, as well as other humans, have. But not without opening my eyes to the walls of the prison. Not without acting as if I had left it. Or as if, in any case, I were able to see it from outside.

In this index an "f" after a number indicates a separate reference on the next page, and an "ff" indicates separate references on the next two pages. A continuous discussion over two or more pages is indicated by a span of page numbers, e.g. "67-70."

Index of names

Index of names